Overcoming Student Failure

Series Titles

Becoming Reflective Students and Teachers With Portfolios and Authentic Assessment—Paris & Ayres

Creating Responsible Learners: The Role of a Positive Classroom Environment—Ridley & Walthers

Motivating Hard to Reach Students—McCombs & Pope

New Approaches to Literacy: Helping Students Develop Reading and Writing Skills—Marzano & Paynter

Overcoming Student Failure: Changing Motives and Incentives for Learning—Covington & Teel

In Preparation

Inventive Strategies for Teaching Mathematics—Middleton & Goepfert

Teaching for Thinking—Sternberg & Spear-Swerling

Designing Integrated Curricula—Jones, Rasmussen, & Lindberg

Effective Learning and Study Strategies—Weinstein & Hume

Positive Affective Climates—Mills & Timm

Dealing With Anxiety in the School—Tobias & Tobias

Overcoming Student Failure

Changing Motives and Incentives for Learning

Martin V. Covington and Karen Manheim Teel

AMERICAN PSYCHOLOGICAL ASSOCIATION | WASHINGTON, DC

Published by
American Psychological Association
750 First Street, NE
Washington, DC 20002

Copies may be ordered from
APA Order Department
P.O. Box 2710
Hyattsville, MD 20784

In the UK and Europe, copies may be ordered from
American Psychological Association
3 Henrietta Street
Covent Garden, London
WC2E 8LU England

Typeset in Berkeley and Bell Gothic by University Graphics, Inc., York, PA
Printer: Data Reproductions, Rochester Hills, MI
Cover Designer: KINETIK Communication Graphics, Inc., Washington, DC
Technical/Production Editor: Sarah J. Trembath

Library of Congress Cataloging-in-Publication Data
Covington, Martin V., 1938–
    Overcoming student failure : changing motives and incentives for
learning / Martin V. Covington and Karen Manheim Teel.
        p.   cm. — (Psychology in the classroom)
    Includes bibliographical references.
    ISBN 1-55798-343-7 (alk. paper)
    1. Motivation in education—United States.   2. Rewards and punishments in education—United States.   3. Educational equalization—United States.   4. School failure—United States.   I. Teel, Karen Manheim.   II. Title.   III. Series.
    LB1065.C656   1996   95-39473
    370.15′4—dc20   CIP

British Library Cataloguing-in-Publication Data
A CIP record is available from the British Library.

Printed in the United States of America
First Edition

TABLE OF CONTENTS

PREFACE

What is the purpose of school? What is the purpose of grades? What are the reasons we as teachers sometimes use an ability-based, competitive grading system? What impact does such an approach have on young people, especially students who lack confidence in themselves as students? These are the kinds of questions we raise in this book.

We have collaborated over the last 6 years in developing and assessing curriculum and evaluation strategies that address the problems of low academic self-esteem and negative motivation in schools. Our work consists of a series of classroom research projects that have involved both university participants and classroom teachers.

Drawing on our individual and joint teaching and research experiences, we will consider the role of incentives in promoting learning and achievement. We look mostly at the formal structure of grading systems and their role as motivators. We will attempt to dismantle various false beliefs about incentives and motivation by addressing the true educational value of incentives: which rewards can best promote learning, and what rewards can do and can't do. Finally, we will show how rewards and incentives can be arranged to encourage learning, thinking, and proper motivation.

As a vehicle for self-reflection throughout the book, we present a series of self-directed questions. Through these questions, we have tried to set up a kind of interactive conversation. The questions ask you to draw on your own experiences as teachers to organize your thoughts around the issues presented. Consequently, we hope that you will see yourself as an active participant.

Most teachers who read this book will have already thought about the issues raised here and may not always find our ideas especially new. However, we hope that the perspectives we offer will assist you in framing the issues in a helpful light and acting on them more effectively.

ACKNOWLEDGMENTS

We are indebted to many individuals who have made this book possible. During the earlier stages of our collaboration, various faculty members and graduate students at the University of California, Berkeley made rich contributions to the development of our thinking and to the many teaching strategies that Karen has used with her students at Portola Middle School. In particular, we recognize Laurie Close, Ramah Commanday, Matt Downey, Cathy McDonald, Sybil Madison, and especially Andrea DeBruin Parecki, who has been an ongoing associate from the start both as a classroom observer and as a data analyst.

In addition, this book could not have been written without the support and encouragement of colleagues in the West Contra Costa Unified School District and particularly at Portola Middle School. We are very grateful to have had the opportunity to test our theories in live classroom contexts. The classroom research conducted at Portola Middle School was supported in part by the National Academy of Education and by a Spencer postdoctoral Fellowship awarded to coauthor Karen Teel. Most importantly, without the cooperation of the students in Karen's classes, we would not have gained the insights we have into the strengths and problems associated with various curriculum ideas and grading strategies.

Finally, we want to express our gratitude to three individuals who provided us with yet a different kind of support. We thank one of Karen's colleagues at Portola Middle School, Gail Harrison, and another colleague who teaches science in the Oakland, California schools, Anthony Cody, for reviewing an earlier version of the book and for giving us invaluable feedback. We also thank Judy Shelton for her patience and expertise in typing and retyping several versions of the manuscript.

introduction

Educational reform is the watchword today. Calls for change are driven largely by concerns over declining test scores and fears that America's youth will not be able to compete successfully in the global marketplace of the 21st century. A variety of solutions have been proposed for reversing the statistics that place American schools near the bottom of the achievement ladder among industrialized nations. Chief among these proposals is a call for adopting more rigorous national achievement standards and holding both teachers and students accountable for attaining them.

In order to implement these higher standards, schools are being pressed to extend the school year, require more homework, and employ more testing. These recommendations for reform have been described as a *policy of intensification* (Russell, 1988)—in effect, simply continuing to do what has been done for years, but more of it. There is much to recommend this proposal of intensification. Clearly, holding high standards is critical to improved achievement; if we expect little of our students, little is what we will get. Yet this solution by itself is insufficient; something is missing. The answer to reform is not as easy as simply raising academic standards or adding new courses. If students are not succeeding now against old, less demanding requirements, increased demands seem pointless. This criticism was put bluntly, if not sarcastically, by a businessman who recently commented,

> If I had a situation in which one third of my products [students] fell off the assembly line along the way [national dropout rate prior to high school graduation] and two thirds of those remaining did not work right in the end, the last thing I would do is speed up the conveyor belt!

Effective solutions to the declining fortunes of many of America's schools lie elsewhere, requiring a shift in our thinking about the concept of motivation. By focusing on motivation we do not mean to imply necessarily that the problem facing schools is a lack of student motivation, even among those youngsters who sit silently in class or for those who dare teachers to teach them. Consider also those students who seem to easily master the complicated rules for survival in environments like America's ghettos and barrios, yet may resist learning the comparatively simpler rules for diagraming a sentence. Actually, for many of these students—the silent, the indifferent, and the resistant alike—the problem is not a

> The problem is not a lack of motivation; students are motivated, but for the wrong reasons.

lack of motivation; they are motivated, sometimes even overmotivated, but motivated for the wrong reasons. Some students are motivated to avoid failure by not participating at all, others to defy a system they believe to be irrelevant to their lives, and yet others to escape being evaluated on a narrow set of abilities and skills.

Any efforts at true reform must first recognize just how pervasive these negative motives are among America's youth, and then arrange schooling in ways that encourage other, more positive reasons for learning. Only then will calls for increased standards and for more time in school have the desired effect.

The reasons for learning, or not learning, depend to an important degree on the kinds of incentive systems that prevail in classrooms. Some incentives, which actually function as disincentives, undercut positive reasons for achieving. Other incentives both encourage achievement and foster the will to achieve.

The purpose of this book is to explore ways that teachers can modify classroom incentives (including methods of grading) in order to encourage positive reasons for learning among their students. Our goal is not limited solely to increasing the quality of student motivation as a way to enhance academic performance. An additional goal, above and beyond increasing achievement per se, is to foster the willingness to learn as an important educational objective in its own right. There has never been a shortage of support for this noble objective. A half-century ago John Dewey commented that "The most important attitude that can be formed [in schools] is that of the desire to go on learning" (1938/1963, p. 48). More recently, the American business community has called for workers who can renew their own learning and "identify problems . . . adjust to unanticipated situations, and work out new ways of handling recurring problems" (National Academy of Sciences Panel on Secondary School Education for the Changing Workplace, 1984, pp. 20–21). If teachers are to take these challenges seriously, the question becomes, "How can teachers arrange classroom incentive systems to promote the will to learn?" This is the essential question we pose and attempt to answer in this book.

Nature and Scope of Solutions Proposed

A few words are needed about the kinds of solutions we will propose. We are convinced that the most constructive and sustainable changes are those initiated by individual teachers and not imposed from above by school boards or by federal or state authority. For this reason, the focus of this book is on what individual teachers can do to improve the academic and motivational quality of classroom life. Obviously, teachers cannot single-handedly counter the enormous problems reflected in low test scores nationwide or statistics such as those indicating that upwards of 30% of America's students do not graduate from high school (Haycock & Navarro, 1988). Nor will any one program be sufficient to stem the tide of mediocrity. Moreover, academic failure is as much the result of children growing up in an unstable environment as it is the fault of any single educational philosophy. Nonetheless, we believe that certain school practices contribute to student demoralization and need be reconsidered by teachers, no matter how modest these problems may be compared to the other overwhelming difficulties facing many of America's children today in the form of drugs, crime, and neglect.

Our recommendations are compatible with current theories of human motivation (e.g., Ames, 1984; Covington, 1992) and represent practical steps that can be implemented without any extraordinary demands on teacher time and resources. This suggests that our thoughts are not especially new, but are familiar enough to be introduced without a major dislocation of the system. Indeed, much of what we suggest is already well known, but simply needs more emphasis and coordination. Our purpose is to place known techniques in a larger perspective provided by modern motivation theory, and in so doing elevate the commonplace to a new order of significance. For teachers already using these approaches or convinced of the need to do so, we hope to provide additional justification for their efforts.

Before proceeding, it will be helpful to preview the general line of argument we will take.

A LEVEL PLAYING FIELD: MOTIVATING ALL STUDENTS

First, we need to define the concept of *motivation*. Basically, the concept of motivation answers the age-old question about the *why* of human behavior: Why, for example, does a student choose to work on one task while virtually ignoring others (*preference*)? Why does the same student work longer and with greater relish on one task than on another (*energy level*)? Why do some students give up working long before others do (*persistence*)?

The answer is that preference, energy level, and persistence all depend on one's reasons (or motives) for learning. For instance, some students learn only for the sake of immediate, tangible payoffs and will quit working when these rewards are no longer available. Other students see school as a "winner take all" contest and will become motivated only when they judge that they can prevail over others. Still other students are drawn to, and captured by, those assignments that call for creativity and self-expression, tasks which in the conventional sense can never be finished. From these examples, one can understand that it is the reasons that students learn that largely determine how much they learn, how well they retain knowledge, and whether the knowledge they gain either enhances or detracts from a sense of self-confidence and the willingness to learn more.

> Preference, energy level, and persistence all depend on one's motives for learning.

We will liken school to a game, albeit a serious learning game, with a complicated set of rules for achievement. These rules largely determine how classroom rewards such as grades, praise, or gold stars are distributed. We will argue, in turn, that the particular reasons for learning that operate in any classroom depend on these rules (Covington, 1992). Many classrooms feature rules that turn schooling into an *ability game*—that is, the promotion of motives not necessarily to learn, but rather to outperform others in an effort to bolster one's reputation for ability—or the promotion of motives to achieve, driven out of the fear that others will do better (Ames, 1984; Ames & Archer, 1987).

These are destructive reasons for learning because they distract students from true achievement, undermine the willingness to try, and promote invidious comparisons among learners. In this circumstance, learning becomes abrasive—certainly not something that one would want to continue for even a day, let alone over a lifetime.

From this perspective, then, the improper use of incentives can create a failure-prone environment in which the playing field is tilted against most students. When fear is the stimulus, there are few winners in the learning game. And even the winners may pay a heavy price.

However, teachers can encourage positive reasons for learning, and thereby establish a level or fair playing field from which all students can approach success. We will refer to this arrangement as an *equity game*. But how can everyone win, and what is it that makes the playing field level? In effect, what is the basis for such equity? Obviously, students are unequal in many ways. Each student enters school from different starting points: No two students have the same talents; nor do all students exhibit the same learning styles. Yet every student can share common reasons for learning. This concept is what we will call *motivational equity*. Everyone can feel the thrill of intellectual discovery, can become caught up in the act of problem-solving, and everyone can experience the satisfaction of self-improvement. Differences in ability, background, and talent are no barriers to these experiences.

> The improper use of incentives can create a failure-prone environment.

These positive reasons for learning are largely intrinsic in nature, that is, the rewards for achieving them reside in the actions themselves. For example, the act of satisfying one's curiosity is its own reward. And because these rewards reside within the individual, they are open to all, inexhaustible in number, and largely under the control of the individual.

From this perspective, the challenge for schools is to create a motivational parity for all students, with everyone striving for positive reasons by arranging incentives that promote curiosity, that establish meaningful payoffs for self-improvement, and that reward increased knowledge.

We will explore two different strategies for promoting motivational equity. The first strategy rewards the efforts of students to master their environment, to progress, and to strive for something better (e.g., "If you figure out the assignment and explain it to the whole class, I will give you 20 extra bonus points."). The second strategy seeks to strengthen the will to learn by rewarding curiosity and information-seeking motives. Intellectual excellence is reflected not only by the number and difficulty of the problems individuals solve, but also by curiosity expressed in the process of identifying and even creating new problems (e.g., "You'll get credit for each additional question you pose whose answer cannot be found in the textbook.").

Creating equity-based incentive systems is not easy. Teachers must address various concerns that arise whenever the idea of encouraging intrinsic motivation is proposed. Several of these issues are important enough to mention in advance. First, assuming that learning is its own reward, when everyone learns it follows that everyone must be rewarded. But are not rewards devalued when everyone wins? In short, who wants to play a game in which everyone wins? Another concern is whether students can ever truly love learning if they are paid to learn in the form of points, credit, or grades. We will take up these issues later.

OVERVIEW OF THE BOOK

Rationale

This book examines classrooms whose reward structure favors an ability game in which students are driven to aggrandize a sense of ability and achieve out of the fear that they are falling behind others. We will explore the devastating consequences of such negative reasons for learning that, first and foremost, cause the destruction of the love of learning. Ability games are based on three wrongheaded assumptions, actually persuasive myths, about the nature of motivation and rewards: (a) Students who do not try in school are unmotivated; (b) achievement is greatest when rewards (e.g., grades) are distributed on a competitive basis, that is, with the greatest number of rewards going to those who perform best; and (c) the greater the rewards offered, the harder students will try. We will demonstrate the falsity of these myths.

We will also explore the positive educational benefits of incentives. Not everything about incentives is counterproductive. In fact, the use of grades and rewards becomes largely negative only when they are part of an ability game. In Goal 2, we will consider how grades and other incentives can be arranged to encourage positive reasons for learning as part of an equity game. An equity game involves rewarding the struggle for self-improvement, not winning over others; promoting effort, not aggrandizing ability; and encouraging creativity, not fostering compliance. In Goal 3, we discuss how to overcome obstacles to instituting this new system of incentives.

> An equity game involves rewarding the struggle for self-improvement, not winning over others; promoting effort, not aggrandizing ability; and encouraging creativity, not fostering compliance.

In a final review, we revisit a classroom that was run according to the ability game, and examine the ways learning might change for the same students in an equity game.

Goals

The lessons to be learned from this book can be stated in terms of the goals to be achieved by the reader, which are:

1. an understanding of the negative consequences of schooling when students are motivated by an ability game to outperform others rather than to learn;

2. an understanding of how grades and other tangible incentives can be arranged to encourage positive reasons for learning under an equity game; and

3. an appreciation for the kinds of obstacles that stand in the way of transforming the rules of the learning game, and suggestions for how to deal with them.

goal one

Understanding the Negative Effects
of the Ability Game

The first goal is to gain an appreciation for the kinds of implicit rules of achievement that turn schooling into an ability game. These rules determine how success and failure are defined—for example, whether or not students succeed by doing better than others. Because grades are the most visible evidence of how well students play the ability game, we start with an analysis of grades and grading policy. Then we introduce a hypothetical classroom in which the ability game has taken root. Using this case study as a starting point, we discuss the myths and problems associated with schooling that is based on the ability game.

KEEPING SCORE: THE CASE AGAINST GRADES

Many kinds of incentives are used in school. They range from highly tangible rewards such as edibles (candy and ice cream) and visible social reinforcers such as teacher praise to intangible rewards that are intrinsic to the act of learning itself, such as the satisfaction of curiosity. And then, ultimately, there are grades that form the vanguard of all school incentives. School grades are central to our story for several reasons. For one thing, grades represent the most widely used index for judging overall success and failure in school. For another thing, grades enjoy great credibility among both parents and college admissions officers. Finally, grades take on an exaggerated importance for many children. Indeed, research indicates that no single thing contributes more to a student's sense of worth than does a good report card, nor devastates it so completely as do poor grades (Covington, 1992). There cannot be much doubt about the importance attached to grades by adults. For instance, the reported incidence of child abuse, including beatings, doubles at the end of each school term when grades are sent home (Toufexis, 1989). Given their significance, grades easily become equated in the minds of youngsters with a sense of worth; in effect, many children come to hold themselves to be only as worthy as their school-related achievements, despite the fact that the grades one gets have nothing to do with whether one is a loving, good, or courageous individual, for example.

> No single thing contributes more to a student's sense of worth than does a good report card.

If grades hold such extraordinary power—not only the power to determine who goes to college and even which college, but more importantly the power to shape one's sense of worth as a person—then they must be taken into account in any serious effort to explore the possibilities of educational reform.

As a first step in this exploratory process, it is important to categorize in advance the various ways that traditional grading methods are a potential threat to students.

We have already implied several reasons for this, mainly that grades can easily become the main yardstick by which one's worth is determined. This yardstick is often applied in an atmosphere of surveillance and unequal power in which authority figures like teachers seek to insure compliance. The encouragement of a sense of positive self-regard in an atmosphere of compliance and inequity is at best an unlikely proposition. Moreover, even the expectation of receiving good grades can put students at risk, especially when students do not get the grade they believe they deserve. In this case, the disappointment acts like a punishment (Kohn, 1986).

SELF-DIRECTED QUESTION

What are some other ways that grades pose a potential threat to learning?

Here are a number of additional concerns about grades and grading often mentioned by teachers:

1 Getting good grades can become more important than learning. Grading also may discourage creativity and intellectual risk-taking.

2 Grades may put students and teachers at odds and create an atmosphere of mistrust and suspicion, whereas true learning can only thrive in an atmosphere of trust and support.

3 Grades may encourage cheating, since students may feel the pressure to outperform others at any cost.

4 Grades are highly subjective and sometimes are not applied fairly or given for the right reasons. For example, grades do not always reflect legitimate educational objectives like the degree of improvement or the final level of achievement attained, but rather often become indications of student compliance and of behaving oneself, and may even reflect teacher favoritism.

5 Grades tend to segregate students into artificial groups reflecting different levels of preparation, or ability groups that form the basis for social stereotypes and prejudice.

If there is so much wrong with grades and traditional grading methods, then why are they employed at all? Can't we simply outlaw grades if they are so bad? All teachers have agonized at times over grades as "necessary evils" and have often wished that grades did not exist. But traditional grades and grading methods still persist and are virtually unchanged from the practices introduced nearly a hundred years ago. So why do these practices continue? There must be reasons.

1 One way to identify these reasons is to envision the world of schooling without grades. What would be missed if grades were banished?

2 How would teachers have to alter their teaching in ways that would compensate for whatever it was about grades that was important?

These questions evoke a wide range of responses from teachers. Here is a sampling:

1 If grades were eliminated, teachers ask, how would they motivate students to learn, especially indifferent students? Without grades, what other incentives would be powerful enough—schoolwork itself? Although some assignments might be worth tackling for their own sake, much of learning is repetitive, even mechanical and boring. Where are the intrinsic rewards in these cases?

2 Without grades, how would teachers reward truly outstanding performances?

3 What about the need to control one's classroom? Doesn't the threat of poor grades help keep students in line? Without grades, wouldn't the power and authority of teachers be badly eroded?

4 For all the problems grades raise, how would students get along without grades? How would students gauge their progress and know how well they were doing?

5 And don't grades help to identify emerging talent? Aren't grades the main way society selects those students most able to take advantage of higher education in a competitive society?

No one is about to eliminate grades, and eliminating grades is not advocated in this book. Grades are here to stay. But the role and meaning of grades and other tangible school rewards can be changed for the better, and in the process can promote greater learning and the will to continue learning. This sampling of teacher responses to the vision of a "gradeless" world lays the groundwork for thinking about changes and underscores the need to consider more than grades and rewards per se. Educators also need to rethink the entire experience of schooling, including the concept of motivation, the curriculum, and the instructional process itself.

Now that we have anticipated this larger perspective, we can shift from a fantasy world without grades back to present reality, where grades form a central part of school life. How are grades and other incentives typically used in schools, and what is their likely impact on teachers and students alike? The following scenario features a fictional middle school teacher, Ms. Jackson, whose educational philosophy and teaching practices represent those observed by us many times in real classrooms. Likewise, the individual students described here are also fictional but typical of many youngsters who are at risk for educational failure. No reference is made to the particular subject matter taught by Ms. Jackson to underscore the point that the dynamics described here occur irrespective of subject content. Finally, although the setting is the middle school years, the issues raised cut across all grade levels.

MS. JACKSON'S CLASSROOM

Ms. Jackson prides herself on a traditional approach to teaching, which includes her views on grades and grading. For Ms. Jackson, grades are an important motivator. She is a firm believer in the proposition that the more praise given or the higher the grades awarded, the harder students will try. Sometimes Ms. Jackson even grades students leniently on the theory that they will work hard to keep a good grade. On the other hand, she may occasionally grade other students harder on the theory that when students experience an unexpectedly poor grade they will work that much more to make it up. Ms. Jackson also defends grades as the best way to recognize and reward outstanding performances, so she usually reserves the top grades in her class for those few students who do best.

Ms. Jackson hopes that her methods of grading will encourage a conscientious attitude toward schoolwork and a sense of responsibility for doing well on assignments, the first time, and on time, qualities which she believes will prepare students for the rigors of economic survival in later life. For this reason she doesn't accept late work, takes points off for mistakes, and does not typically allow her students to redo assignments.

In Ms. Jackson's view, the future success of her students also depends on learning the value of competition. Although she herself is not competitive by nature, Ms. Jackson believes in healthy competition—that is, competition in small doses as a way to encourage students to do their best. For example, she occasionally gives higher grades to those students who finish their assignments first.

Ms. Jackson is also mindful of the need to give everyone a chance to feel successful, not just the top two or three students or those who finish first. So sometimes she gives a good grade to anyone who completes an assignment satisfactorily.

Ms. Jackson feels that she is supportive of her students and their struggle to attain personal excellence, and attempts always to maintain a friendly, open, and accepting manner. In short, Ms. Jackson believes herself to be rigorous but fair, an opinion shared by her fellow teachers.

We step into the life of Ms. Jackson's classroom at a revealing moment. For the past 2 weeks Ms. Jackson's students have been studying for a test that they just took yesterday. Now, as Ms. Jackson passes back the corrected tests, there is a variety of reactions to the grades circled in red at the top of the page.

Noel

Noel turns pale, obviously distressed by her grade of "C" because she knows "A"s and "B"s are important. She begins nervously to glance around to see who did better and who did worse. Noel is a paradox. Grades are important to her, but she is her own worst enemy. It seems to Ms. Jackson that Noel would rather find excuses for not studying than to study even a little, and lately Noel has taken to procrastinating in her work. These days, Noel rarely turns in assignments on time and gives the excuse that she had too much else to do. She also does not settle down to study until the last possible moment. Ms. Jackson tries to help Noel turn things around by giving her a second chance, something Ms. Jackson does not ordinarily do, by offering to extend the deadlines on several assignments. However, Noel waited until the extended deadlines had almost passed before beginning work.

[To the reader: Replies to the following self-directed questions are found throughout this book in subsequent sections.]

1 Ms. Jackson knows Noel is afraid of getting poor grades, so Ms. Jackson reasons that, out of fear alone, Noel should try harder. So why doesn't Noel take advantage of Ms. Jackson's offers of help?

2 And why does Noel continue to procrastinate and put things off, which actually sets up the very failures that she seems to fear?

Sean

Sean is a bright, conscientious, and compliant youngster—a model straight-"A" student. Ms. Jackson knows that Sean has studied hard for this test, as he always does, which may be the reason that he appears to be devastated by the "B+" he receives. Sean fidgets, tapping his fingers on the desk, and stares off into the middle distance, distracted and anxious. Ms. Jackson is puzzled by Sean's overreaction to his grade. After all, a "B+" is one of the best grades in the room and besides, Sean is still getting an "A" in this class. Ms. Jackson tries to reassure Sean to no avail. He seems so nervous and unsure of himself when it comes to schoolwork. For Sean, nothing is fun about learning.

1 Why should Sean be so upset over this one temporary setback?

2 Another thing puzzles Ms. Jackson about Sean. Why isn't Sean enjoying himself, given his many successes?

Lydia

Lydia doesn't even bother to open up the test. From the look on her face it seems that she must know, or at least fear, her grade. After making sure no one is watching, she wads up the test and sticks it in her pocket. She smiles ruefully as if to say, "Out of sight, out of mind." But is it? Ms. Jackson has worried about Lydia's lack of progress ever since she was transferred into her class several months ago. She seemed so withdrawn. Ms. Jackson suspects that Lydia has become apathetic because of her past failures in school. Ms. Jackson attempts to compensate for the past by redoubling her praise of Lydia whenever she turns in homework or attempts to participate in class. At the same time, Ms. Jackson tries to ignore Lydia's test failures on the reasonable assumption that Lydia is already more than aware of her shortcomings. But nothing seems to help. Lydia doesn't even take advantage of those assignments for which she, like everyone else, can get a good grade by simply trying hard. Ms. Jackson is doing everything she can to encourage Lydia, but with little success. Nothing she has tried seems to work.

1. Lydia doesn't respond to increased praise. Why not? Shouldn't praising students for their effort strengthen their willingness to try harder the next time and increase their sense of self-confidence?

2. At the same time, ignoring Lydia's failures doesn't seem to help much either. Why not?

3. Additionally, why doesn't Lydia reach out for those successes that are clearly within her grasp? She may be demoralized by past failures, but doesn't this mean that she should be all the more ready to seize on success when it is offered?

Michael

Michael sprawls nonchalantly at his desk, as if to say, "I don't care about the grade." And apparently he doesn't. After glancing briefly at his test, he goes back to running his pencil aimlessly around the grooved initials in the top of his desk, carved long ago by some other, probably equally turned-off student. For Michael, taking the test was an empty gesture anyway, because he has been either tardy or absent so much lately that he can't catch up now even if he wanted to. It isn't that Michael is a troublemaker or behaves disruptively in class, but it is something almost worse: he is sullen—even morose—and he appears utterly indifferent to classroom activities.

To all outward appearances, Michael is unmotivated. However, Michael might be highly motivated, but for the wrong reasons. What might these reasons be?

SCHOOL AS AN ABILITY GAME

Every classroom has an implicit set of rules that conveys information to students about how they are to be judged and what they must do if they hope to be successful. These rules can be thought of as a kind of game, actually a very serious game (Abt, 1987). First, like all popular games, classrooms have a scoring arrangement by which players (students) receive points or credit (e.g., praise or grades). Second, there are obstacles that must be overcome to gain points. Sometimes the obstacles are other students with whom the individual competes for a limited number of good grades. Other times the obstacles are the classroom assignments themselves. Third, there is the matter of who makes up the rules and enforces them. Typically, this is the teacher. Although this game analogy to classroom learning is not exact, the parallel is close enough to provide us with some important insights regarding Ms. Jackson's students.

The rules by which Ms. Jackson requires her students to play support an ability game. In an ability game, students often come to equate getting good grades with being worthy; in other words, one is thought to be only as good as one's ability to achieve. Thus, in this game the ultimate goal is to aggrandize one's reputation for ability, and high ability is demonstrated by outperforming others or by achieving noteworthy successes with little or no effort. Good grades are valued, then, not necessarily because they mean that one has learned a lot but because they imply that one is able, whereas poor grades imply a lack of ability that triggers feelings of worthlessness.

This scramble for high test scores and the superior ability status that high grades imply occurs because of the way Ms. Jackson's students keep score. Recall that Ms. Jackson reserves the highest grades for those students who do best, which is defined by her as doing better than others on tests or learning faster than others with a minimum of errors, not necessarily doing well in terms of self-improvement, learning to recognize and correct one's mistakes, or being conscientious in one's studies. Yet because some students learn more quickly and perform better than others, the inevitable result is fewer rewards for those who perform less well but who still may be performing at their best.

The perceived importance of ability is promoted further by Ms. Jackson's view that learning should be efficient, with a minimum of mistakes. In effect, many of her students come to believe that smart pupils don't make mistakes, but dumb ones do. Also, as ability becomes more important in the eyes of her students, the kinds of ability thought necessary for success inevitably narrow to verbal and abstract reasoning skills. Clearly, Ms. Jackson is right in emphasizing the development of linguistic skills that are central to economic survival in adulthood, namely the abilities to read and comprehend what one reads and to communicate one's ideas in writing. However, by focusing on ability narrowly defined, Ms. Jackson increases the potential for stratifying her students. Actually, there are many ways to communicate one's ideas (Gardner, 1993). Ideas can be communicated in verbal form, in dramatic or musical form, in a visual mode, or through kinesthetic channels (those skills highly developed in actors, athletes, dancers, and craftpersons). Ignoring these nontraditional ways to express what one has learned limits the ways students can succeed.

> In an ability game, the obstacles to success become other students.

In an ability game, the obstacles to success become other students. In the scramble for high grades, some students will do virtually anything to succeed or to prevent others from succeeding. One strategy is to sabotage the efforts of other students. This happens only infrequently at the elementary or middle grade levels, but acts of sabotage are widespread in high school and college, where students steal assigned books from the library or rip out crucial pages in an effort to foil others. However, the biggest opponent by far is the teacher, because it is the teacher who sets up the rules by which students must play. As a result, in an ability game the teacher–student relationship is basically power oriented, with the teacher exercising authority over students.

Other practices not necessarily portrayed in Ms. Jackson's class, but quite frequently observed in schools, also sustain those dynamics by which success is defined around perceived ability. One involves the practice of assigning students to different reading or math groups within a class defined by levels of proficiency, from a low track to a high track. Such groupings encourage the view that a lack of ability causes poor performance. By contrast, when students work in groups not necessarily defined by skill levels, limited skills are seen as less important to success, especially among those groups that cooperate in achieving a common goal (Weinstein, 1981).

These same criticisms apply to ability grouping across whole classrooms, especially the demoralizing effect on youngsters in the lower tracks. At this point in time, there is no convincing evidence that tracking of this kind accelerates achievement compared to the progress of comparable students in mixed-ability classrooms (Oakes, 1987; Slavin, 1987). Moreover, when it comes to emotional reactions, the evidence is decidedly negative, with students in lower tracks demonstrating unreasonably low aspirations and negative attitudes towards school (Alexander & McDill, 1976).

Then consider the widespread practice of having all students work simultaneously on the same assignment. Such an arrangement accentuates differences in the rate at which students work that translate into assumptions about ability, with slower students presumed to be less able when, in fact, they may be less prepared or may possess a learning style conducive to accuracy rather than speed (Rosenholtz & Wilson, 1980).

Finally, ability dynamics are further accelerated by the practice of maintaining sharp boundaries between academic and nonacademic work. When what counts as academic assignments becomes narrowed to only a few activities or comes to depend on a narrow set of skills, the potential for stratification of perceived ability increases.

At this point it may be helpful to summarize the basic characteristics of an ability game. In an ability game:

1. Success is defined by high grades and performing better than others.

2. Value is placed on ability narrowly defined, not on effort.

3. The main source of pride is doing better than others.

4. The obstacles to success are other students.

5. The teacher is a judge.

6. Making errors and mistakes is considered to be evidence of stupidity.

THE DYNAMICS OF SELF-WORTH

There is a tendency in our society to equate achievement with human worth. In effect, people are held to be only as good as their achievements, and in schools these accomplishments typically depend on a narrow set of abilities (Covington, 1992). And, because good grades in Ms. Jackson's class depend so heavily on certain abilities and on doing better than others, her students are especially likely to confuse ability with worth. In short, to be able (in the ways *able* is defined in Ms. Jackson's class) is to be worthy, but to do poorly compared to others seems evidence of inability and thus reason to despair of one's worth and give up. Equating high grades (and the ability to achieve them) with one's personal worth is a risky step because in an ability game only a few students can succeed. This means that, rather than striving for success, many children are forced to avoid failure, and if they do fail, they may feel compelled to avoid the implications of failure by giving excuses.

A number of failure-avoiding strategies have been identified by researchers (Birney, Burdick, & Teevan, 1969), most of which are only too familiar to teachers. We list several of the most frequently observed of these strategies:

■ *Nonperformance:* The most obvious way to avoid failure and its implications for low ability is simply not to participate. This strategy takes many forms: appearing eager to answer the teacher's question, but gambling that the teacher will call on someone else who appears more reluctant; scrunching down in ones's seat to avoid being seen by the teacher; and avoiding eye contact, hoping to make as small a target for the teacher's gaze as possible. In themselves, these minor deceptions are innocuous enough. Nonetheless, they may portend other more serious, chronic kinds of noninvolvement, such as dropping out and excessive absenteeism.

- *Sham Effort:* In order to avoid being criticized for not trying, students will sometimes appear to participate, but participate less in an attempt to succeed than in an effort to avoid teacher punishment. Again, there are many variations on this theme: students asking a question even though the answer is already known to them; adopting a pensive, quizzical expression; and feigning rapt attention during a class discussion.

- *Procrastination:* By postponing study for a test until the last moment, individuals can blame failure on poor time management, thereby deflecting attention away from the possibility that they are incompetent. A variation on this theme involves those students who take on so many jobs that they can never give sufficient time to any one project.

- *Impossibly High Goals:* By setting one's aspirations very high—so high that success is virtually impossible—students can avoid the implication that they are incompetent because most everyone else is also likely to fail against such odds. This reasoning explains why students who are low in self-confidence can sometimes perform better when the odds seem against succeeding. These students can now work up to their capacity without fear, because if failure does occur it no longer necessarily implies low ability because no one else could do better.

- *The Academic Wooden Leg:* Here, individuals admit to a minor personal weakness—the proverbial wooden leg—in order to avoid acknowledging a greater feared weakness such as being incompetent. One example is to blame a failing test score on test anxiety. Having test anxiety is not as devastating to a personal sense of worth as is accepting inability as the cause of the low score.

By understanding these premises, several conclusions can be drawn that illustrate the falsity of the myths about motivation and rewards mentioned earlier.

QUESTIONING MYTHS ABOUT MOTIVATION

Three Pervasive Myths

Myth: Students Who Do Not Try in School Are Unmotivated.

According to a self-worth analysis, many students described as indifferent, reluctant, or lazy are not unmotivated at all but actually may be overmotivated, but for the wrong reasons. They are expending great energy in an effort to protect a sense of worth, but in self-defeating ways rather than by pursuing worthwhile accomplishments, which ultimately is the only firm foundation on which self-esteem can grow and flourish. This analysis underscores the bankruptcy of the idea of school reform based on a policy of intensification that would rely on raising the stakes in an already-losing game by requiring more compliance and stiffer penalties for noncompliance. According to self-worth theory (Covington, 1992), a change in the reasons for learning is needed in order to reduce student belligerency and truancy, and to reverse low achievement.

Myth: Achievement Is Greatest When Grades Are Awarded on a Competitive Basis.

When students compete for diminishing rewards or for only a few good grades, as in Ms. Jackson's classroom, learning is the first casualty. It is true that scarcity of rewards may set students to scrambling for a time, especially among those students who believe that they have a good chance to win. But in the long run, most students will do virtually everything except learn in their attempts to avoid having fewer points than others. This dynamic is described by Alfie Kohn (1986) in the following terms: "How can we do our best when we are spending our energies trying to make others lose—in fear that they will make us lose?" (p. 9)

Myth: The Greater the Rewards Offered, the Harder Students Will Try.

In an ability game, ironically, trying hard can threaten a sense of the student's worth (Covington & Omelich, 1979). This occurs because when students study hard and fail anyway, the implication is that they are not very able. This puts students in a dilemma about whether to try or not. On the one hand, teachers reward hard work. On the other hand, trying hard and losing implies low ability. Furthermore, perceptions of incompetency trigger feelings of shame and humiliation, and sometimes anger and resentment.

Thus when "push comes to shove," students often must choose between risking a reputation for competency and passing up the rewards offered by the teacher for trying hard. In these circumstances, many choose not to try or if they do try, do so unenergetically and with excuses always handy (Covington & Beery, 1976). There is little wonder, then, that trying to motivate students to greater effort by grading them leniently, as Ms. Jackson does occasionally, has little impact on student performances, nor does grading harder on the theory that when students experience an unexpectedly poor grade they will work more to make it up. These grading policies are ineffective because they do not take into account the underlying motivational dynamics of students.

More specifically, in an ability game effort is threatening no matter how the teacher arranges rewards. The irony is that grades tend to motivate those students who least need motivating, that is, those who are already successful, whereas, perversely, the very students who need motivating the most (i.e., failing students) are most put off and threatened by grades. Successful students are motivated by both positive and negative feedback, whereas the poor student often meets an unexpected success with disbelief, if not suspicion, and a bad grade simply confirms his or her low self-image.

Analyzing Noel, Sean, Lydia, and Michael

This self-worth analysis of Ms. Jackson's classroom also helps us better understand the reasons for the reactions of Noel, Sean, Lydia, and Michael to their grades.

Noel

Like many middle-class students, Noel has tied her sense of worth to getting high grades. As a result, she is always comparing herself to other students, which is a notoriously poor yardstick for gauging the quality of one's efforts and the degree to which one is improving and learning. In order to avoid feelings of worthlessness, Noel has unwittingly created a number of excuses for why her mediocre performance should not be attributed to incompetency, but rather be explained by factors beyond her control. Recall that Noel has begun procrastinating in her work assignments, thereby virtually ensuring a low grade. Her failure, however, is failure with "honor," that is, a failure that reveals little about Noel's ability because no one could be expected to do very well when there is so little time to prepare.

Noel's excuses may temporarily forestall the shame and sense of worthlessness that accompany a disappointing performance, but tragically, in the long run Noel is setting up the very failures she also fears. This is why she is only getting "C"s, not "B"s and "A"s, of which she is quite capable.

Sean

A self-worth analysis also helps make sense of Sean's apparent overreaction to a disappointing, yet still very respectable grade of "B+." Sean's reaction typifies the plight of those students whom self-worth theorists refer to as *overstrivers* (Beery, 1975; Covington, 1992). Overstrivers are students who fear failure every bit as much as do *failure-avoiders* like Noel. Both Sean and Noel share a common fate by having linked their sense of worth to outperforming others. But Sean and Noel's ways of coping are different. Noel evades feelings of worthlessness by creating excuses for her disappointing performances. Conversely, Sean has chosen unconsciously to avoid the feelings of failure by succeeding. Unfortunately, this strategy is just as destructive as the one pursued by Noel, even though in the short run Sean can boast an exceedingly high grade point average. For overstrivers, even extraordinary successes do little to resolve lingering doubts about their ability. This is the reason that a single isolated "failure" like Sean's "B+"

can be so devastating. Here failure simply acts to confirm what Sean has always feared—that he really isn't capable enough—because his goal is not merely doing well but being perfect!

Lydia

Like all youngsters, Lydia needs a chance to do well and feel successful, but it is not always clear how teachers can help, and common sense is not always the best guide.

First, consider Ms. Jackson's strategy of praising Lydia for her successes. Shouldn't praise reinforce the will to learn? Not always. It all depends on the reasons for the praise. If Lydia believes that her success is due to an easy task, then praise will do little to increase confidence in her ability to achieve (Covington, Teel, & Parecki, 1994).

Praise is also problematic for another reason. When praise is given in an ability game, it acts less as a recognition of one's accomplishments and more as an endorsement of the person complying, with the hidden message "I will reward you because you did what I asked you to." In this context, praise increases the student's dependency on the teacher as the dominant source of the student's sense of worth and confidence. In an ability game there is little opportunity for students to create their own internal standards as to what counts for excellence.

Second, consider Ms. Jackson's strategy of minimizing or downplaying Lydia's failures by withholding criticism. Ironically enough, this practice, which makes perfect sense otherwise, may give Lydia the impression that Ms. Jackson expects little from her academically (Graham, 1988). This paradox arises because withholding blame (or giving a bad grade) implies that the cause of doing badly was not insufficient effort—otherwise Ms. Jackson would have reprimanded Lydia because teachers take a dim view of not trying. Thus, by the process of elimination, the cause of Lydia's failure must be low ability!

Third, why would Lydia not undertake those assignments that literally guarantee success for everyone? In an ability game when everyone wins, the task is likely to be perceived by students as a relatively easy one certainly not requiring any great ability. Such successes are devalued because they do little to aggrandize one's reputation for ability. Thus, in this circumstance, all students, including Lydia, are less motivated to seek out rewards that are available to everyone.

At times it appears that teachers cannot win no matter how hard they try to encourage their students. But again, things go badly not because teachers are insensitive or uncaring, but rather because they do not always address the underlying motivations of their students.

Michael

Noel, Sean, and Lydia all share an allegiance to an entrepreneurial spirit that fuels a scramble for improved social status, the aggrandizement of ability at the expense of others, and a preoccupation with high test scores for their own sake. By contrast, Michael, like many youngsters, finds these mainstream, competitive values at odds with his goals that lie outside the realm of traditional academics. Michael derives his sense of worth more from helping his family, from maintaining a tight-knit neighborhood tradition, and from becoming self-reliant in an attempt to benefit his family and community (Stack, 1974). Moreover, the ways that Michael prefers to achieve these goals are alien to the more traditional competitive values that emphasize individuality. Michael prefers cooperation and sharing. As a result, if Michael is to play the learning game, he must play by rules that are foreign to him.

Little wonder that Michael distances himself from what he sees as a losing battle. This process, referred to by Claude Steele (1988) as *disidentification*, is made all the easier by a growing belief that the lessons to be learned in school are irrelevant to Michael's life.

If many schools in America pose a dilemma for students in the ways we have described, then responsible attempts at school reform need to consider ways to make the rewards of learning more compatible with the needs of all children. This does not mean lowering the standards of academic excellence. Whatever else we might say, all youngsters must eventually come to terms with traditional, mainstream American values and acquire marketable skills in order to make a living. Also, skill requirements of the curriculum should not be watered down to accommodate the lowest common denominator of student performance, which simply reflects the school's minimum expectations for some youngsters. Rather, educators must arrange school learning so that it encourages more varied achievement goals than those associated narrowly with competitive excellence. Furthermore, the means by which students achieve excellence, including an emphasis on group problem solving and cooperation, must be broadened. Above all, schooling must be changed from being a competitive game in which those few students who are best prepared in certain skill areas are rewarded most to a game where sufficient rewards are available so that all students will be encouraged to approach success and do their best, rather than merely to avoid failure.

IN DEFENSE OF MS. JACKSON

The drift toward an ability game in Ms. Jackson's classroom is quite common and often occurs despite the best intentions of teachers. There are several reasons for this.

First, the myths about the value of competition for motivating students and the presumption that teachers can control students' achievement by increasing rewards are widely accepted in our society as basic articles of faith. They appear to be consistent with common sense and everyday experience, which makes them even more difficult to dislodge. For example, what could be more sensible than to expect individuals to comply more vigorously the more rewards that are offered?

Intellectually, it is difficult to give up these beliefs even when classroom experiences have proven them to be false. Giving up the beliefs means recognizing that teachers have less "muscle power" for controlling their students than is often thought to be the case and that the use of grades as motivators is not effective for all students. One of the major fears of teachers is that they may lose control of their classrooms. What teachers need, many will tell you, is more, not less, power. In this respect, Ms. Jackson has become victimized along with her students by seductive, but wrongheaded, beliefs about the power of grades to motivate students. This raises the prospect that any genuine educational reform must promote a different kind of relationship between teachers and their students, one that replaces the traditional approach by which teachers hold power over students by reason of grades.

Second, the competitive process by which Ms. Jackson's students sort themselves according to perceived ability cannot be attributed solely to the nature of schooling. Individuals naturally compare themselves to one another when they are trying to establish their place in the world, whether in or out of school (Suls & Miller, 1977). Nowhere is this truer than in the case of judging one's ability, beginning in the earliest years. Primary-grade children usually make judgements about their ability against a standard of self-improvement and often express satisfaction at how much they are learning, irrespective of how well others are doing. However, in time, such self-appraisals give way to comparing one's rate of progress against that of others. This kind of progression from less to more competitive comparisons appears to be a natural one, but it can get out of hand and interfere unduly with learning unless teachers take direct steps to counter the more destructive features

> Any genuine reform must promote a different kind of relationship between teachers and students.

of these comparisons. Thus, if Ms. Jackson can be faulted at all, it is not for consciously encouraging competition, but rather for not taking steps to curb the more excessive forms of competitive comparisons.

Actually, if properly used, comparisons can help facilitate learning in much the same way that long-distance runners often pair up in their efforts to set world records, with one runner setting a pace that the other runner must surpass in order to break the record. We now know that judging one's progress by how well others are doing can actually benefit learning as long as other kinds of comparisons are made available (Butler, 1993). More beneficial comparisons include providing examples of different but permissible ways to work on a problem, or samples of work reflecting various standards of quality, from mediocre to superior, thus providing standards against which everyone can compete (Butler, 1993). It is when social comparisons are the only or the dominant source of self-evaluation that falling short becomes a threat to one's sense of worth.

Third, not all we have criticized about Ms. Jackson's methods so far is necessarily wrong. Consider the practice of ability grouping. Criticizing the segregation of students by ability does not mean that we can disregard the reality that students differ in ability. For example, in order to maximize the motivation to learn, teachers need to provide the opportunity for students to work on tasks that are neither too hard nor too easy, given their current achievement levels and skills (Woodson, 1975). However, ability grouping is not the way to achieve this kind of balance. Grouping by ability comes to grief not because the goal of providing instruction according to student ability is wrong, but rather because when grouping is employed in an ability game, ability *differences* invariably become equated with *deficits*. We must seek ways to encourage the special qualities of each student while recognizing that ability differences are part of that uniqueness.

Far from dismissing or minimizing the importance of ability, we will soon argue that teachers must actively promote positive beliefs about ability that sustain motivation, not beliefs that create feelings of deficiency and worthlessness. Beliefs about ability that best promote learning involve an elastic view of ability—in short, ability conceived of as an expandable set of skills that improve and grow through experience and instruction. Students who embrace this so-called *incremental* theory of ability are more likely to show greater involvement in school, and are less preoccupied with learning as a test of their worth (Dweck & Bempechat, 1983). A contrasting, widely held notion of ability is the so-called *entity* theory of ability. According to this theory, ability is thought to be a fixed amount or quantity—in short, an immutable capacity of largely genetic origin that is unresponsive to instruction or improvement. Believing one's ability to be fixed is a potentially debilitating step because if a student judges his or her performance inadequate by reason of low ability, there is little that can be done to correct the situation. Interestingly, as students grow older, starting in the middle elementary years the incremental view of ability is gradually replaced by an entity belief. This change in beliefs is accelerated by the introduction of competitive reward structures (Harari & Covington, 1981).

The teacher's job in response to these realities is to foster student beliefs about the truly flexible, multidimensional nature of human talent (see Goal 2, Step 3).

Fourth and finally, teachers like Ms. Jackson are caught in a trap not of their own making, but one that reflects the largely contradictory demands that society places on schools. Schools are expected to function both to teach students and to segregate them, that is, in this latter instance, to identify those youngsters who are likely to profit the most from further instruction. This function is part of the larger sorting process by which all individuals are eventually allocated proportionately to the available jobs across society, some of which (the fewest number) are the most prestigious or lucrative.

> The nurturing of talent and the selection of talent are essentially incompatible goals.

The nurturing of talent and the selection of talent are essentially incompatible goals, and teachers are caught in between. When learning is the goal, teachers view mistakes and errors as a healthy part of the process and allow their students to redo their work. But when teachers take on the responsibility of insuring high test scores, they tend to use autocratic teaching techniques and encourage competition in an effort to energize students. The fact that most teachers see student learning, not student selection, as the more legitimate goal of schooling simply intensifies the conflict.

The conflict of purpose between the selection and the nurturing of talent is well illustrated by the research of Kaplan and Swant (1973). Whenever teachers were told that the student's task was to learn something new and learn it well, teachers universally identified *effort* as the most important ingredient to success. In contrast, when these same teachers were asked to nominate those students whom they believed most likely to succeed in prestigious jobs, they universally favored *ability* as the dominant criterion. Not surprisingly, youngsters deduce that although effort is admirable, it is ability, and especially ability narrowly defined, that counts most in the wider society. Although ability certainly does count, so too do other attributes when it comes to striving for the best one can be: dedication of effort, curiosity, persistence, and a love of learning over a lifetime.

If there is a common theme in these obstacles facing Ms. Jackson, it is that the odds are against establishing positive reasons for learning whenever instruction occurs in an ability-based climate. It is also important to note that like all climates that are psychological in nature, an ability-based climate also resides in the minds of individuals and may not always be perceived in the same ways by everyone. For example, Ms. Jackson was not particularly aware of the dynamics of the ability game that controlled her students, although she was acutely aware of the consequences of this game as reflected in the puzzling behavior of Noel and the others. However, because students are the players in the learning game, they may sense things about the achievement climate that are not always readily apparent to teachers.

STUDENT ACTIVITY: QUIZ

It may prove instructive for teachers to ask their students to identify the degree to which they believe themselves to be playing an ability game. The following set of statements may be useful for this purpose. The statements are arranged around various themes that characterize ability-oriented classrooms and are intended to provoke student responses on various issues.

These statements can be administered in different ways. For example, they can be modified in the form of brief essay questions that students can answer anonymously, or they can be used as the basis for a class discussion if anonymity is not an issue. Not all items need be used, but the teacher should draw on at least one statement from each category in order to gain a complete picture.

1 SUCCESS DEFINED COMPETITIVELY

In this class only a few students can get good grades, even though everyone may try their hardest.

In this class most students are not recognized for doing good work.

2 FEARS ABOUT INABILITY

In this class students worry that they will look dumb.

Students worry about not being smart enough in this class.

3 GRADES VERSUS KNOWLEDGE

In this class students worry more about getting good grades than about how much they learn.

In this class the grade is more important than knowing a student did his or her best.

4 | PERCEPTIONS OF ERRORS AND MISTAKES

In this class making mistakes is not okay, even when students learn from them.

In this class students are not allowed to correct their mistakes.

5 | ABILITY VS. EFFORT

Trying hard does not count for a lot in this classroom.

Being bright is more important than trying hard.

6 | USING MULTIPLE ABILITIES

In this class I do not have much chance to use my special gifts and talents.

Students do not have much choice in this class about how to do assignments.

PAYING FOR PERFORMANCE

Probably nothing both saddens and infuriates teachers more than the question from students, "Do I have to know this for the test?" It saddens teachers because such remarks herald the breakdown of the true mission of education—encouraging a love of learning, not just learning to pass a test. The question infuriates teachers because it often arises despite their best efforts to help students take the high road toward excellence.

Like most teachers, Ms. Jackson also has had her fill of students learning only what is absolutely necessary, and has grown weary of the endless rounds of arguing with students, and sometimes even with parents or family members, over why the grade isn't higher. Such "grade grubbing" has a common origin in the fact that good grades become scarce in an ability game, and poor grades reflect badly on one's worth. In effect, children become desperate and scramble for any advantage they can wheedle. There is another factor that contributes to this nitpicking. Whenever students are offered good grades as a reward (or as a way to motivate them, as Ms. Jackson does), the students tend to operate expediently and succumb to what researchers call the *mini-max principle*, that is, they attempt to maximize rewards with a minimum of effort (Pittman, Boggiano, & Ruble, 1983). This atmosphere of expediency is counterproductive for several reasons.

First, students like Noel tend to choose easier tasks, not only to get away with as little effort as possible (Harter, 1981), but also because expending little effort while risking failure is less threatening. Besides, working on easy tasks guarantees at least a minimum of success.

Second, when the goal is to maximize rewards for a minimum of effort, students adopt conservative learning strategies and are no longer content to take the kind of intellectual risks associated with the satisfaction of curiosity or learning for the sake of discovery. Taking the easy way out is especially crucial for overstrivers, like Sean, who must always win in order to protect a sense of worth. When learning becomes an adventurous process, mistakes and errors are inevitable, even necessary. However, it is these same errors that are interpreted as evidence of failure when the mini-max strategy prevails.

Third, and perhaps worst of all, this sense of expediency interferes with intrinsic motivation. This point is well documented by research: Providing people with tangible rewards for what they would otherwise do freely or just for fun turns play into work, and even drudgery (Lepper & Greene, 1978). This happens because an already justifiable activity becomes suspect by the promise of additional rewards so that students reason, in effect, "If someone has to pay me to do this, then it must not be worth doing for its own sake."

Once again, we can appreciate the sense of drudgery and dread that pervades Sean's feeling about school, even though on the surface he appears to be doing exceedingly well. For Sean, learning has become a way to obtain good grades in order to avoid failure, not a way to satisfy his curiosity or to discover something of interest. This explains why learning is neither fun nor adventurous for Sean.

Clearly, there is much about learning that can, and should, be playful—discovering, exploring, and creating. There is also much about learning that is work, but hopefully it is meaningful work defined by such qualities as persistence and dedication of effort, and by such phrases as "good work" and "pride in workmanship." A balance must be maintained between play and work before the will to learn can be strengthened and sustained over time. Unfortunately, in an ability game play is turned into work of the worst kind—work perceived as a chore to be completed under threat of failure.

SUMMARY

This motivational analysis of classroom life has led us to the conclusion that a great deal of school learning is characterized by student apathy, resistance, and, above all, fear—fear of losing and of being judged as incompetent. As a result, students are driven to pursue negative incentives for destructive reasons, such as the desire to win over others or to position themselves to avoid the implications of failure, even though such maneuvering ultimately creates the very failures that are so threatening. This climate creates a highly noxious situation because the dominant reinforcers are negative. That is, success is counted largely in terms of avoiding something that is bad, not necessarily achieving something that is good. These circumstances detract from true learning and focus students' attention on performance per se, without regard for what is learned or its meaning to one's life. Thus, above and beyond those distractors to learning that exist outside of school—homelessness and hunger, child abuse, and urban violence—there remain many negative elements within the fabric of the school structure itself.

If there is as much wrong with grades and grading as there seems to be, then what are teachers to do? Grades are a fact—indeed, a way of life. School boards require them, parents expect them, and society uses grades to sort students into different jobs and career paths, some of which are more prestigious and valued than others. In short, grades and grading have become a part of our institutional lives. Teachers cannot be expected to defy such entrenched traditions. Grades and grading are here to stay. So the question becomes, "How can grades and other rewards be used to motivate students for positive reasons, such as learning for its own sake, or to acquire knowledge that benefits others?" Answering this question means that teachers must encourage different kinds of excellence, but at the same time they must make certain that the resulting diversity does not unduly threaten the individual. Nowhere has this point been better made than by John Gardner (1961) when he asked, "How can we provide opportunities and rewards for individuals of every degree of ability, so that individuals at every level will realize their full potentialities, perform at their best, and harbor no resentment toward any other level?" (p. 115).

> How can grades and other rewards be used to motivate students for positive reasons?

The answers to this question will be taken up next. In anticipation, we can say, once again, that grading and the use of rewards become largely negative, not because of anything inherently unhealthy about the process of evaluation or wrong with rewards per se, but because all too often grading and evaluation take place in the context of schooling conceived of as an ability game. Therefore, we need to change the rules of the learning game, and in the process grading and evaluation will become a more positive feature of classroom life. This transformation involves the shift to an equity game.

SUGGESTED READINGS

Covington, M. V. (1992). *Making the grade: A self-worth perspective on motivation and school reform.* New York: Cambridge University Press.

Cuban, L. (1990). Reforming again, again, and again. *Educational Researcher, 19,* 3–13.

Gardner, J. W. (1961). *Excellence: Can we be equal and excellent too?* New York: Harper & Row.

Sarason, S. B. (1990). *The predictable failure of educational reform: Can we change course before it's too late?* San Francisco: Jossey-Bass.

Schorr, L. B. (1988). *Within our reach: Breaking the cycle of disadvantage.* New York: Anchor/Doubleday.

Stipeck, D. J. (1988). *Motivation to learn: From theory to practice.* Englewood Cliffs, NJ: Prentice-Hall.

Weinstein, R. S. (1989). Perceptions of classroom processes and student motivation: Children's views of self-fulfilling prophecies. In R. E. Ames & C. Ames (Eds.), *Research on Motivation in Education* (Vol. 3). New York: Academic Press.

goal two

Changing the Rules: Activities to Promote Positive Reasons for Learning

What is an equity game? An equity game involves rules that establish a level playing field so that all students can feel successful in school and strive for something better, irrespective of how well or poorly other students are doing. In this goal, the steps that constitute an equity game are examined, using coauthor Karen Teel's class to demonstrate the success of this system. Activities are also suggested to inspire teachers' attempts to institute an equity plan.

There are at least five kinds of equity that promote individual excellence and help avoid the negative dynamics of the ability game. These sources are listed below.

Components of the equity game:

- insuring equal access to rewards

- rewarding mastery and curiosity

- rewarding multiple abilities

- offering alternative incentives

- making assignments engaging

FIVE STEPS TO INSTITUTING AN EQUITY FOCUS

Step 1: Insuring Equal Access to Rewards

First, equity means providing all students with an equal opportunity to do well. This involves revising the rules of the learning game so that students are rewarded for the quality of their work measured in absolute terms. That is, students are rewarded based on whether their work surpasses or falls short of the standards of excellence set by the teacher or by students themselves, not rewards based on whether one student does better than another, as in the case of an ability game. Most school assignments can be cast in absolute terms and have numerous counterparts in the outside world. Consider the 15-year-old preparing to pass her driver's test, or the second-year medical student studying to pass an examination that will certify him as a pharmacist. In theory, anyone can become a licensed pharmacist, although of course in practice, not everyone will choose a career in pharmacy or be capable of the challenge posed by the requirements of a pharmacy license. The point is that no one is precluded from trying, and their success does not depend on how well or poorly others do. Similarly, in an equity game, rewards are accessible to all students, as long as they take up and meet the challenge set by the teacher.

Step 2: Rewarding Mastery and Curiosity

Second, equity means establishing a common basis in the reasons that students learn. Everyone can strive to do something better, to improve, and to experience the satisfaction of doing things for him- or herself. These reasons for learning are open to all students—they are a second source of equity, and provide a powerful source of pride within the grasp of all. Feelings of pride act as powerful self-reinforcers and sustain the will to learn. In an ability game, pride depends on aggrandizing one's ability status, or on outsmarting the teacher. But when failure (doing less well than others) threatens one's self-image of ability, students are likely to withdraw from learning. In contrast, by shifting to an equity game, pride comes to depend less on winning and more on persistence, on the quality of one's effort, and on improvement. In an equity game these qualities are rewarded directly and as a result, they become internalized so that pride in accomplishment sustains learning even though others may be learning faster.

Step 3: Rewarding Multiple Abilities

Third, equity means arranging the learning game so that all can put their best foot forward and be judged on their strengths and on what they know or can do well, not necessarily for what they don't know or cannot easily express. This kind of equity involves rewarding the expression of one's ideas and thoughts through any of a number of different modes of ability, say, by illustrating a concept through pantomime (bodily-kinesthetic ability), by creating a diagram (visual ability), or by devising a time line (spatial ability). In this sense equity means honoring many kinds of human ability, not ability defined solely around verbal and abstract reasoning, as is typical in the traditional ability game.

Step 4: Offering Alternative Incentives

Fourth, equity means offering alternative incentives for learning of equal motivational value to all students. Sometimes tangible payoffs may be offered initially to encourage students to learn, until pride in their accomplishments becomes self-reinforcing. To be effective, such incentives must be personally meaningful to students, and students value incentives differently. Some students respond best to social approval, while others value tangible prizes, and still others prefer privileges such as free time or an opportunity to browse in the school library. Creating an equity-of-incentive value involves matching individual students with preferred rewards.

Step 5: Making Assignments Engaging

Fifth, equity also means providing school assignments that are inherently engaging for all students, apart from any tangible payoffs they might receive for working on them. Engaging assignments share certain characteristics. First, such tasks are novel and offer an element of surprise, a common stimulant for all students. They also build on each student's own personal interests. Finally, engaging assignments are inherently appealing to the extent that they are relevant to each student's world.

All five of these sources of equity go hand in hand, and together they encourage the will to learn and continue learning, in part because rewards are plentiful and meaningful. Also, the reasons for learning in an equity game are positive and open to all, and the more students learn, the better able they are to solve the problems that intrigue them and that hold personal relevance.

We (your coauthors) have studied the processes by which classrooms can be transformed from an ability game into an equity game (Teel, Parecki, & Covington, 1992; 1993; Teel, Covington, & Parecki, 1996). Although we have concentrated on achievement among learners at risk for educational failure in the middle school years, the principles we have been testing can be applied with little modification to most other youngsters of all ages.

Our attempts to create equity incentive systems have evolved over the past 5 years, sometimes on a trial-and-error basis, but always guided by theory and buttressed by the commonsense observations of participating teachers and collaborating staff, students, and faculty from the University of California at Berkeley. One research strategy is to start the school year with classrooms structured competitively. Then at the beginning of the second quarter, the rules of the learning game are changed to an equity focus for the remainder of the school year. In this way we can compare any benefits of an equity game against an initial baseline of school as an ability game. This procedure was used in the classroom experiment described below.

IMPLEMENTING NEW REWARD STRATEGIES: KAREN TEEL'S CLASSROOM

We will now consider each of the five steps that transformed Karen's classroom, and suggest ways that other teachers can make similar changes in their own classes. These suggestions are presented in the form of specific classroom activities, many of which we developed as part of our research program.

What kinds of equity incentive systems have evolved to date? This question is best answered by stepping directly into the classroom life of an actual 7th-grade world history class taught by coauthor Karen Teel.

It is a Monday morning at the end of the second quarter, approximately 2 months after the equity rules were introduced, and time to settle up accounts for the final grade for the quarter. Karen has just gone over a list of the quarter's assignments, of which the students have been keeping their own records. Karen's reminder sends students rummaging around in their folders, where several already completed but long-forgotten assignments are found and quickly turned in. Other students scurry to complete past-due assignments amidst the vocal protests of several students who insist that they did, indeed, turn in their "missing" assignments. This checklist follows (see Exhibit A).

EXHIBIT A	2nd-Quarter Checklist of Assignments and Grading Scale

NAME _____

POINTS
POSSIBLE

1. 3 research questions of your choice about Songhai— an African kingdom in the middle ages   10

2. Chart on 3 African kingdoms based on pictures in your text   20

3. Current events #1   10

4. Reading card #1   5

5. Songhai project   50
    A. Answers to 3 research questions
    B. Creative project (booklet, drawing, imaginary letter, etc.) based on your 3 questions

6. Map activity—3 African kingdoms   15

7. Worksheet/hidden word puzzle—3 African kingdoms   25

8. Essay on computer, 1st draft—3 African kingdoms   40

9. Assignment sheet   10

10. Essay on computer, final draft—3 African kingdoms   40

11. Current events #2   10

12. Starpower game   50
    A. Score sheet describing 4 days
    B. "Wrap-up" questions

13. Current events #3   10

14. Current events #4   10

15. Reading card #2   5

16. African country project, 1st draft—to include: 100
    A. "P.C. Globe"
    B. Goal sheet—information from the computer program, describing what you will do and how you will use your time in class
    C. 4 topics (either from P.C. globe or from other references), drawings, skit/song/rap, or brochures

17. Current events #5   10

18. Reading card #3   5

19. Maya worksheet (map & questions)   25

20. African-American biographies (10 of them)   50

21. Homework—activity based on Maya pictures in text   25

22. Country project, final draft (all corrections on 1st draft)   125

Total possible points for assignments = 650

Cooperation points = 150

Total for quarter = 800

As can be seen from this checklist, missing even a few assignments can make all the difference between a good and a mediocre report card because the final grade depends on how many points each student accumulates over the quarter: so many points for an "A," so many points for a "B," and so on. Every point counts! Students get points for everything they do, from the simplest and briefest of tasks to those more rigorous and complex research projects that extend over several weeks. Karen's students have come to realize in the span of only a few months that in order to do well they must compete, not against one another as in an ability game, but against the standards set by Karen. So, in theory, everyone can do well. There is equal access to rewards (points) if students will just work for them. As one student described Karen's approach,

> See, like most teachers or a couple of teachers, if you miss assignments, they won't tell you, and they just mark you an "F" for it. Most teachers won't try to tell you to come in and make it up 'cause, like, if you have a "B" in Ms. Teel's class and you missed a major assignment or a couple of assignments, and you find them out, and do everything she wants you to do and you'll keep your grades up in that class.

However, even though everyone can win in Karen's class, she is no less demanding than is Ms. Jackson in what she requires in exchange for a top grade; it is only the means by which their respective students succeed that distinguishes these two teachers. For Karen, rewards are earned largely by being conscientious and by drawing on a variety of personal skills, whereas being successful in Ms. Jackson's class depends largely on the ability to compete with others.

Karen controls both the quality and quantity of work required in her class by a simple rule: The better the grade students want, the more they must do and the better they must do it. This does not mean that every student will do equally well. Some of Karen's students struggle more than others on reading and writing assignments due to initially poor skill levels. In order to motivate these students to do their best, irrespective of how well others are doing, Karen gives a substantial amount of grade credit for how much students improve and for making progress. Improvement is rewarded when students redo assignments for additional points after they receive corrective feedback, even though the work might have been of passing quality the first time. Because everyone can improve, this becomes a source of motivational equity. One adult classroom observer noted,

> Karen talked about the test. She said that the grade was important, but that it was not final—it represents what you did that first time. "I encourage you to do it over to raise your grade . . . . You can fix it, so don't be discouraged."

Students can also earn points toward their final grade by participating in the intellectual life of the class—by answering questions, expressing their curiosity, raising questions, and sharing what puzzles or intrigues them about the subject matter being taught. In this way Karen reinforces another positive reason for learning and a source of equity for all—learning for the sake of discovery and for the satisfaction of curiosity.

Credit is also given for being planful, and for analyzing in advance how difficult the various assignments are likely to be. Here, difficulty is measured not with reference to one's peers, that is, "hard for me compared to others." Such a comparison is an open invitation to become preoccupied with one's ability. Karen measures difficulty against a yardstick of "hard or easy for me," which implies the opportunity to exercise and extend one's own mastery, irrespective of how well or poorly others are doing. A case in point occurred on Tuesday morning, when Karen introduced the first major assignment of the new quarter. She asked the students to pick their own African country and required that they write a report due in 2 weeks. Karen encouraged students to begin planning their reports and to think about what was difficult about this assignment for each of them personally, and discuss among themselves how they would deal with these difficulties. She gave students the rest of the class period to come up with their ideas. A good plan would be worth 10 extra-credit points.

Another classroom observer described the resulting discussion as follows:

> There was great participation in this discussion about the purpose of the project [to learn about Africa], what the end product would be [a tour guide], and how to find information about the topics [in books provided]. Alvin and Charisse suggested that the travel guides Karen gave them would show how to organize their books. Neomia and Charisse also talked about helping others in the group by sharing information they might find on another's topic. The group also felt that pictures were very useful in providing ideas, and helping people to understand about other cultures. Students love it when they are given the opportunity to speak about something they know and understand.

At first, shortly after the equity rules were introduced, some students had a difficult time making the connection between hard work and good grades. This happened because in their earlier years, try as they might, these youngsters still did poorly compared with others, which meant bad grades even though they did their best. But by this point in the equity game, most students had caught on. Hard work was beginning to pay off. This message was reassuring and made learning safer. Students now found themselves responsible for their own grades, depending on how hard they chose to work and how much they chose to do. One student made this point forcefully: "I already [raised my grade] in Ms. Teel's class. A 'B' is good enough. But now in my other classes . . . I need to work much harder than what I am now."

This sense of control was strengthened by allowing students various choices: choices of assignment and choices of different ways to complete an assignment. Another student remarked,

You probably can do something better if you draw a picture or do a skit or talk about it. If you have a choice, then you really want to do it, and you can express yourself more in what you are trying to do.

On Thursday Karen passed out the final grades for the second quarter: 11 "A"s, 11 "B"s, 8 "C"s, and 1 "D." This was far better than the first-quarter grades given under a competitive ability game: 9 "A"s, 5 "B"s, 5 "C"s, 11 "D"s, and 1 "F." Clearly, most students caught on to the new system of rewards and were thriving; certainly, there was less reluctance and more enthusiasm now. Students knew exactly what was required of them to do well. As another student put it, "We've gotten used to what you expect of us, and we do it." Yet another student explained his attitude this way: "I tried harder—perseverance."

The students were also showing signs of increasing self-confidence, which was a major shift from the first quarter under an ability game, when they seemed far more listless and unsure of themselves. Here are two excerpts from observers' notes in Karen's class:

> I left the room and came back and Maurice came running over to me. He told me with his arms up in the air and a great big smile that he had a "B." He has this intense energy now to get all of the work in and do as well as he can. This is certainly a different child from last quarter. Before he just sat and stared. Now he is totally engaged in the work.

> Olivia has come a long way since September. She seems to try to do her work and shows her assignment sheet willingly to me. She gets angry with herself if her grade is not at least a "C." This quarter she seems to be willing to try.

However, while the entire group improved, there were still big differences in the final grades. Some students earned far more points than the minimum necessary for an "A," whereas several others were still struggling to hang onto a "C." However, as time has gone on, these grade differences seem to recede in importance compared to grading under an ability game when the differences were often a source of resentment and demoralization. For Karen's students, their source of academic self-worth is slowly shifting to qualities within the reach of all—pride in doing well, doing things for oneself, and becoming the best one can be. This transformation can be seen in the kinds of questions that Karen's students asked about their second-quarter grades. In the beginning, under an ability game, many complained about their low grades, yet they showed little inclination to do much about it. Now most of these same students were asking themselves why they weren't getting "B"s and "A"s, and they seemed willing to work toward these new goals with some confidence.

For the remainder of this goal, we will consider each of the five steps which transformed Karen's classroom, and suggest ways that other teachers can also make similar changes in their own classes.

STEP 1: INSURE EQUAL ACCESS TO REWARDS

In an ability game, when students tie their sense of worth to the ability to outperform others, there is no guarantee that they will ever feel successful, no matter how well they do academically, because others may do even better. This makes learning a scary proposition. The first step toward making learning safe is to deal directly with the threat posed by a scarcity of rewards. All students must have access to plentiful rewards, assuming of course that they have earned them.

Basically, the transformation from limited to plentiful rewards requires that teachers judge the achievement of their students in absolute, not relative, terms. In this way, success and failure come to depend on whether or not each individual's performance satisfies the teacher's stated requirements, and not necessarily on how well one does relative to others.

One of the best known examples of an absolute criterion approach to achievement is the merit badge system employed by the Boy Scouts of America. In order to get a merit badge in, say, first aid, youngsters must satisfactorily complete a series of well-specified, discrete requirements, including, in this particular example, an explanation of the dangers of moving a badly injured person. For some requirements, demonstrating one's understanding of first aid is the primary criterion, as in recognizing the most common signs of heart attack. In other instances the practical application of one's knowledge is paramount, as in making an arm-sling or demonstrating CPR satisfactorily.

> **When students tie their sense of worth to the ability to outperform others, there is no guarantee they will ever feel successful.**

These are some ways that the Boy Scouts use absolute criteria in awarding merit badges, but how might these criteria be incorporated into individual assignments and even into the entire curriculum in classrooms? Here are some examples:

EXAMPLE 1 A school assignment using absolute (or merit) criteria: Consider Karen's African country assignment mentioned earlier. She determined that the report must include a number of facts about the country that students learned from the computer program, P. C. Globe. In addition, students were expected to draw a map of their country and of their country's flag. These requirements were couched in absolute terms. Anyone who completed them satisfactorily would get full credit. In this particular case, credit took the form of points. Points were given students for providing the necessary number of facts and for the presence of the map and flag, accurately represented. Naturally, scoring could be more elaborate. Karen might have chosen to place more emphasis on the flag portion of the project and elaborate the task, for example, by permitting students to write a brief essay explaining the symbolism in the flag. The same kinds of elaboration are possible for the map, with points available for including the capital city of the country, locating various rivers, or indicating elevations.

EXAMPLE 2 Criteria by which teachers might judge any school assignment in absolute terms, irrespective of the subject-matter content or the type of assignment:

- *Being on time*: "You'll receive 10 extra points for turning work in on time" (positive reinforcement). "I will subtract 10 points for every day an assignment is late" (negative reinforcement).

- *Length of product:* "Your essay should be more than 100 words, but not longer than 200."

- *Number of ideas:* "Think of four different reasons why the fish died in the fish tank."

- *Quality of ideas:* "What were the three logical steps the debater took to arrive at his conclusion?"

- *Proper outline, following directions*: "Anyone will get 5 extra points if he or she follows the steps in the experiment exactly."

These criteria are simple enough to understand in the abstract. This does not mean, however, that demands stated in absolute terms must themselves be simple. We should not equate clarity of requirements with mediocrity or minimal standards. Even minimums can sometimes be highly demanding. For example, every state has licensing procedures to insure minimal competency among many professional groups. Any number of individuals can be licensed as a psychologist, for example, in a given year in the state of California, as long as each applicant meets or surpasses stringent standards of specialized knowledge and general intellectual functioning.

EXAMPLE 3 An entire curriculum or course of study, not just one assignment, arranged around the concept of absolute criteria: One possibility involves the method around which Karen organized her history class.

Students are given a series of assignments (see assignment checklist). Each task is worth various amounts of credit toward a final grade, with more points available for more complex assignments or for those deemed most crucial to the overall understanding of the course material. Points are awarded for both quality and quantity of work using the kinds of absolute criteria outlined under Example 2.

At the heart of this system is a preannounced schedule by means of which the total points accumulated for each student are converted into the final course grade, so many points for an "A," so many for a "B," and so on. In effect, students can work for any final grade they initially choose, or continue to strive for an even higher grade. The catch is that the higher the grade to which students aspire, the better they must perform on a greater and greater number of tasks. In this way the system rewards persistence and effort, while at the same time permitting quality control by the teacher.

In addition to addressing the issue of scarcity, there are several benefits to a grading system based on absolute standards. First, absolute grading systems have enormous potential for altering the teacher–student relationship from one which, under the rules of the ability game, is largely adversarial and destructive, to one in which the teacher becomes an ally and helpmate to students. The teacher first sets the boundaries for what students must do and how well they must do it. Then, given these challenges, the teacher helps students strive to do their best.

Second, absolute grading systems allow students to exert some control over their own learning, thereby empowering them as confident learners. More specifically, once teachers set the conditions for work and the quality of workmanship, it is the actions of the students, not those of teachers, that control the rewards.

Third, absolute grading systems help solve the problem of praise. As will be recalled, far from motivating students to greater achievements, praise may actually increase student dependency on the teacher as the main source of validation. This alternative approach to grading allows for the distribution of rewards based on the specific strengths and weaknesses in a student's performance as judged against absolute criteria. This kind of feedback creates a condition of *encouragement*. As contrasted to praise, encouragement says, in effect, "Here is how you are doing, and here are some additional ways to do even better next time." It is well known that such messages encourage self-confidence and accelerate achievement (Page, 1958). Such feedback need not always be positive to be effective. Feedback that points out mistakes and weaknesses in one's approach can also accelerate learning, as long as students have the opportunity to improve (Butler & Nisan, 1986).

Fourth, when teachers reward students for performance judged against absolute criteria, even a disappointing grade has the potential to motivate students to try harder next time, because this kind of shortcoming implies falling short of a goal, not falling short as a person (Kennedy & Willcutt, 1964).

Fifth, the use of absolute standards creates a sense that grading is fair, far more than when grades are based on competitive sorting (Covington & Beery, 1976). Perceptions of fairness are an important ingredient in any effort to motivate people. Not surprisingly, individuals become resistant, resentful, and even outraged when they have no choice but to work under a system that they believe to be innately unfair or that gives preferential treatment to some individuals over others.

Sixth, the use of absolute standards requires that students be told precisely what it is that is required of them, how much they must do, and how well they must do it. Knowing what is expected, how best to get there, and how far one has to go is essential to effective learning and to the will to continue learning. In the absence of sufficient structure, students—especially those we have identified as failure-prone like Noel—perform poorly; things worsen when ambiguity and uncertainty occur in an atmosphere of competitive evaluation. Without informational feedback, fearful students expect the worst and tend to prejudge their performances as unacceptable. They fall victim to their own sense of inadequacy and, as a result, become overly dependent on the judgement of others regarding the value of their work.

STEP 2: REWARD MASTERY AND CURIOSITY

By themselves, plentiful rewards are no guarantee that students will seek them out. Not all students will necessarily surpass the requirements for a top grade, especially if these requirements are stringent and complex. Recall the experiences of Ms. Jackson, who found to her dismay that many of her students could not pass even a relatively simple task at a minimally satisfactorily level, despite the absolute nature of the grading. More than the mere availability of rewards is needed. The reasons (motives) for learning must be put right. In an ability game, the reasons for learning promote deception and subterfuge as well as mediocre performance, if not an outright refusal to learn. In an equity game, the reasons for learning encourage the will to learn more, to improve, and to explore. These latter reasons are intrinsic in nature, which means that the rewards reside in the actions themselves. For instance, satisfying one's curiosity is its own reward. Likewise, overcoming a challenge creates pride, and pride in turn becomes a powerful reward (reinforcer) that sustains further learning. Moreover, intrinsic rewards are inexhaustible—open to all and under the control of the learner. Teachers can create a common, absolute basis for recognizing and rewarding students for becoming the best that they can be and striving for something better. In effect, then, even students whose academic progress is slower than others can be sustained in their work—first, because their reasons for learning provide their own built-in rewards, and second, because these intrinsic reasons for learning can be further reinforced by the teacher.

In this section, the manner in which teachers can directly reward the mastery motive is considered. The mastery motive can be divided into three components: rewarding improvement, rewarding realistic goal setting, and rewarding planfulness. Following a discussion of the mastery motive, the ways teachers can strengthen the curiosity and information-seeking motive will be explored.

Mastery Motive

It is human nature to strive for something better, to produce a result as good as the last one, but quicker, and to discover or invent new ways to do old things better. The drive for self-mastery is an important motivational tool if teachers choose to take advantage of it. Unfortunately, it is often the case that the process of self-mastery is underrated or ignored in schools. For example, students are not typically given an opportunity to develop and then refine products or ideas of which they can be justly proud. A typical procedure is to assign one set of materials to be learned, followed by a test, and then the introduction of new material, with little or no opportunity to make up any shortcomings uncovered by the original testing. Leaving material half-mastered not only results in lower grades than might otherwise be obtained after additional effort or practice, but such grades are of the barest help in providing proper guidance about how well students are doing, how they can improve, or how far they have yet to go. Moreover, not being allowed to make up one's deficiencies before proceeding creates a perpetual sense of frustration and a feeling of falling farther and farther behind with no chance to catch up. So why should one continue to try?

> Anyone can persist, struggle, and endure, qualities available to all—an important source of motivational equity.

Rewarding Improvement

When students are given extra chances to improve—to make up deficits and to redress errors—ability no longer predicts the final level of learning students can achieve. What replaces ability as the better predictor is degree of student effort, persistence, and even doggedness. Anyone can persist, struggle, and endure, qualities available to all—an important source of motivational equity. Students are usually willing to redouble their efforts as long as they continue to improve and feel they are

> The struggle now focuses on the task itself, not on competing against others.

making progress. In effect, then, progress itself becomes a positive reinforcer, and so does pride in one's gains.

How might classroom assignments be structured so as to reward students when they improve or are striving for something better?

ACTIVITY 1 **African country report I:** Recall, once again, the African country report that Karen assigned her students. In order to encourage a thorough mastery of the material and provide an opportunity for her students to improve their writing and composition skills, Karen required two drafts of the report: a rough draft and a final version. Karen read over the rough drafts, made suggestions for improvement, and then returned the drafts to her students. Students were expected to make the recommended changes—changes involving the correction of grammatical errors as well as improving content coverage—and then resubmit the improved report. Students received grade points for the rough draft based on its content only. These points were then augmented by additional credit given for improvements in grammar and content shown in the final version.

ACTIVITY 2 **Product improvement:** A variation of the theme on improvement involves presenting students with an adequate but undistinguished example of a completed assignment and then discussing ways to approach the task in a more creative and ingenious fashion, in effect, to improve the product. A related possibility is to provide students with various landmarks of success in the form of sample answers to a question that the teacher might label *beginner*, *intermediate*, and *expert*. If students have access to sample answers that vary in quality, then it becomes that much clearer just how a particular performance will be graded and how students can improve the quality of their replies.

ACTIVITY 3 **Spiral improvement:** Teachers can also provide students with direct evidence of their academic growth over substantial periods of time. One possibility involves a *spiral* lesson plan. An assignment is spiral if it is reintroduced from time to time so students can judge for themselves how much more sophisticated their reasoning is now compared to before, with the strong implication that what may seem perfectly adequate ways of thinking for the present moment will eventually appear just as naive as do their first attempts.

Toward the end of the school year, one teacher assigned a paper topic that was vaguely familiar to his students: "Write a two-page essay on poverty. Why in America, a land of plenty, is there so much poverty?" "It *should* be familiar!" exclaimed a student. "You gave us the exact same assignment months ago." "No matter," replied the teacher, "do it again." The next day the teacher passed back the students' original work on this same assignment done earlier in the year. He also circulated a checklist containing several entries, including the following: (a) Number of ideas explaining the *causes* of poverty; (b) number of suggestions for *solving* the problem of poverty; and (c) number of *facts* describing poverty. He then asked his students to compare the two essays for signs of improvement in each of these categories. Most students found several ways in which their second essay was superior to their first efforts, a circumstance that provoked a lively discussion about what caused the changes.

Rewarding Realistic Goal Setting

A critical element in the struggle to become the best one can be is setting realistic goals. Human beings are inveterate goal-setters, and when individuals achieve their goals, they feel successful and react with pride. Conversely, when they fall short of their goals, they experience failure, and depending on the circumstances of the failure, can experience feelings ranging from self-recrimination and anger to a renewed commitment to try again, but harder next time. The important point here is that success and failure are psychological concepts. They mean different things to different people; indeed, one individual's failure can be another's success, despite the fact that both performed equally well. Thus, some individuals actually create a life of failure, not because they deliberately choose to do so, but because it is the inevitable result of their misguided efforts to bolster a sense of worth by setting admirable, but unrealistically high goals for themselves. In this case the mere statement of a worthy goal, and not its actual achievement, becomes the source of gratification (Sears, 1940).

When individuals are free to explore on their own, they typically place their goals at or near the upper bounds of their current skill levels. Conversely, when they fail to achieve their goal on a given try, they temporarily set their goals lower. In this way, individuals are able to balance the need for insuring social approval by striving for something better with avoiding repeated failures. The net effect is that aspirations spiral upward, usually slightly ahead of current achievement, but not so far ahead that these temporary goals cannot be attained through effort and practice.

Not only is realistic goal-setting critical to mastery; it is also a skill that can be taught and rewarded directly. In what ways can such rewards be introduced into the instructional process?

ACTIVITY 4 | **The spelling bee:** Consider the epitome of all classroom competition—the spelling bee, in which there is one winner, several near-winners, and lots of losers. By introducing only modest changes, as Richard de Charms did (1957, 1972), this game can be transformed into an object lesson in the importance of recognizing and working within one's limits. Students are given a choice of three kinds of words to spell: easy, moderately difficult, and difficult. Students receive 1 point for spelling an easy word, 2 points for spelling a word from the moderately difficult list, and 3 points for the most difficult. The scale of difficulty can be tailored to each individual. Easy words are those that the student has spelled correctly on a previous test; moderately difficult words are those he or she previously misspelled but had an opportunity to correct in the meanwhile; and hard words come from the next spelling assignment that no one has seen yet.

By changing the rules by which youngsters are rewarded, success for de Charms's students came to depend on a careful evaluation of their skill levels—in this case spelling skills—and on a realization that if students disregard their current strengths and weaknesses, no matter how good they are, they may penalize themselves by failing. Thus, the role of ability in achieving success is reduced and is replaced by a source of equity open to all—making realistic appraisals of one's current skill levels. Moreover, students learn that a realistic goal is the most challenging kind—easy enough to insure some level of success, but difficult enough to avoid boredom, and focused on the task itself, not on competing against others. Of equal importance, it is the actions of students themselves in seeking out a manageable goal that determine how accessible the rewards are, not the actions of the teacher or the achievements of other students.

ACTIVITY 5 | **Predicting outcomes:** A goal-setting component can be introduced into any testing situation, irrespective of the subject-matter content. Before starting to study for the test, students can be shown sample items and encouraged to predict how well they will do on the upcoming test (e.g., number of problems solved, number of words spelled correctly). Then, in addition to giving grade points based solely on how well students subsequently perform on the test, the teacher can also award points on the basis of the accuracy of their predictions. The closer the student's predictions are to the actual outcome (either above or below the test score), the more grade points are awarded.

Research has shown that such predictions quickly become the student's learning goal, and because accuracy pays dividends, students tend to set their goals at or near the upper reaches of their current skills and knowledge (Alschuler, 1973). The mere act of setting goals, whether they are rewarded in the ways described above or not, stimulates student achievement by giving students something to strive for. Additionally, goal-setting promotes an interpretation of success as being the result of hard work, not of ability per se, and students feel most satisfied with the results of those assignments on which they have worked hardest, irrespective of the particular grade they receive (Sofia, 1978).

ACTIVITY 6 | **Custom testing:** After studying the passages from a textbook assignment, teachers can give their students a pool of questions from the text whose answers range from easy to difficult. Answering each question satisfactorily is worth so many points, with harder questions worth more points than easier ones. Students are allowed to select any of, say, 10 questions to answer from this pool. The students' grades will depend on how many total points they accumulate over the 10 items they select.

The use of such *custom testing* results in higher test scores than those scores achieved under the traditional method of requiring all students to answer the same questions, thus reflecting a truer estimate of what students have learned (Rocklin & O'Donnell, 1986). These benefits are especially great among failure-prone and test-anxious students, because the negative effects of anxiety are moderated when learners have some control over what they are tested on. Motivationally speaking, students learn with greater enthusiasm when they know that their grades will depend more on what they know, compared to their grades being calculated in negative terms, that is, based on what they don't know. Counting successes, not mistakes, makes a big difference.

ACTIVITY 7 | **Giving students choices:** A variation on custom testing involves giving students a choice as to how much each of several assignments or tests will count toward their final grade. For example, when given the choice of dividing 50 points among five different tests, John, an 8th-grader, chooses to assign 20 points to the test covering the material that interests him the most. On the other hand, Suzy gives greater weight to the assignment she feels most competent to undertake. Once again, the idea is to maximize opportunities for students to feel successful on their own terms and in their own ways.

A related possibility is for teachers to retain control over how much each assignment is worth, but allow students to decide on which of the assignments they wish to receive extra feedback or more in-depth teacher comment. Students are likely to do their best on assignments which they themselves target for extra review by the teacher.

| **ACTIVITY 8** | **Checking progress:** Another variation on customized testing permits students at any

point in their studies to judge for themselves what they have already learned, and to identify those areas where more study is needed, all before they are tested. The teacher creates a set of sample test items on 3" × 5" index cards of the kind to be included on an upcoming test, with several possible answers listed on the back of each card, ranging in quality from mediocre to excellent. After each study session, students choose several cards at random from the deck to create their own self-test. After students answer each question, they compare their answers to those found on the back of each card.

Such feedback is essential for accurate goal-setting, not only for judging how well one is likely to do, but also for gauging when one knows enough to pass at various levels, from minimally acceptable to superior. Encouraging students to check their progress from time to time—say, after each study session—not only promotes a sense of improvement, but is also an excellent way to hone one's self-monitoring skills when it comes to deciding how best to study and what remains to be worked on. In this connection, most students—even college students—exhibit surprisingly low levels of comprehension monitoring while they read. For instance, college students who are given passages to read that contain difficult paragraphs tend to read through these difficult sections without slowing down.

Rewarding Planning Ability

The ability to plan is another important skill component of the motive for self-mastery. Good planning involves a capacity for self-monitoring, that is, recognizing one's intellectual strengths and weaknesses and preferred ways of thinking. For example, students who possess accurate skills of self-monitoring realize that some things are harder for them to do than other things, and because they are planful in their thinking, these students also know how to compensate for their weaknesses (McCombs, 1984). Good planners also are adept at estimating how much time and effort will be required to complete assignments, and to think in terms of the steps needed to achieve these objectives (Neimark, Slotnick, & Ulrich, 1971).

> Counting successes, not mistakes, makes a big difference.

Good planning also has important motivational consequences. For one thing, good planners believe that ability is incremental and, as we already know, incremental beliefs about ability are associated with a willingness to tackle difficult problems. For another thing, if students analyze assignments for various sources of difficulty, develop plans to overcome these obstacles, and still do poorly, they are likely to attribute a poor job to reasons other than low ability—like poor planning—thereby freeing themselves to work harder and correct their errors.

Fortunately, there is considerable evidence that being planful can be promoted directly in school (Covington, 1986). One of the best ways for teachers to do this is to employ *contingency contracts*. Contingency contracting involves establishing work contracts between individual students and teachers. Typically, such work contracts include a clear statement of what the student is to do, the time at which the work is to be completed, and the kinds of rewards or payoffs that the student can expect. The term "contingency contracting" refers to the fact that the rewards are contingent on the successful completion of the contract. Setting work deadlines, agreeing about how much will be accomplished, and choosing what standards will prevail requires thoughtful planning and foresight.

Work contracts can vary widely in their scope, complexity, and duration. For example, a brief microcontract

EXHIBIT B	Work Contract

Name _____

A. For this assignment you will do the following, as agreed upon by you and your teacher:

1) _____

2) _____

3) _____

4) _____

B. You have agreed to turn this assignment in by this date: _____

C. If you complete this assignment according to the requirements we have agreed to, you will receive a grade of _____

D. Write down what you will try to do on this assignment each day:

Day: _____
_____

Day: _____
_____

Day: _____
_____

Day: _____
_____

_____   _____
Student signature   Teacher signature

may involve mastering only one small step in the process of learning a larger operation, such as diagraming sentences. Then there is the longer-term contract, the completion of which depends upon coordinating the many intervening skill steps involved in, say, long division.

We have included an example of a work contract in generic form that can be modified easily by teachers to fit different age groups and any number of specific assignments or circumstances (see Exhibit B).

Contingency contracting fulfills several of our guidelines for effective incentive systems. First of all, contingency contracting is noncompetitive. Here success or failure depends on the plans and actions of the individual student. Second, contingency contracting communicates the expectation that all students will complete their work successfully, not just a

EXHIBIT C	Task Analysis Questionnaire

Name _____

Assignment _____

1. What do you have to do to complete this assignment?

_____

_____

_____

_____

2. What will be *hard* about doing this assignment?

_____

_____

_____

3. What will you do to make the hard part easier?

_____

_____

4. What do you think you will enjoy most about this assignment?

_____

_____

_____

few. Third, contingency contracting promotes greater certainty regarding what is expected of students, thus reinforcing a task orientation where the emphasis is on accomplishment rather than seeking praise or avoiding the teacher's disapproval. Fourth, if properly negotiated, contracts establish a match between the student's present skill level and the demands of the assignment, thus avoiding the frustration and anxiety of working beyond one's current ability, in which case failure is likely. One also escapes the boredom of working beneath one's ability level, an equally debilitating situation. Rather, an optimal match insures that effort and persistence are the two main ingredients in success, since the agreed-upon work is within the present capabilities of the child. Achieving such a match depends on a proper *task analysis*. Students must analyze their work assignments to determine what, if anything, makes the tasks difficult, and then take steps to overcome these potential problems, as Karen does with her students.

Rewards that favor strategic planning and proper task

analysis can be made part of virtually any classroom assignment, irrespective of the age of one's students or the subject-matter content, as indicated by the following sample task analysis questionnaire (see Exhibit C).

ACTIVITY 9 | **Making hard things easier:** As a practical example, consider the typing teacher who gave a final course grade based on points accumulated by her students reflecting the number of words correctly typed per minute on a series of increasingly difficult passages (Alschuler, 1969). When students reached typing levels beyond their present skills, the teacher encouraged them to inspect carefully and analyze these passages, identify difficult strokes and letter combinations, and then discuss solutions with other students who had already negotiated these difficulties successfully. These students not only quickly improved, but in the process also learned how to make a difficult task easier.

Taking a planful approach to learning therefore has several advantages. First, making hard things easier focuses attention on the true obstacles to learning, that is, the complexity of the task and the current limitations of the individual's skills. Second, simplifying tasks improves the chances for succeeding without necessarily lowering one's aspirations. Third, there is less reason for students to avoid trying hard for fear that it will reflect badly on their ability should they fail. In this case, failure, even after much effort, may occur because of an improper task analysis, because students simply gave up too soon, or because they set their aspirations too high. All of these interpretations are within the student's power to correct, and strengthen the student's sense of being the agent of his or her successes.

ACTIVITY 10 | **Planning:** Being planful, in this case conducting a good task analysis, is critical to all effective learning. Consider the lack of planfulness when it comes to solving arithmetic word problems. Many students mindlessly add, subtract, multiply, or divide without first deciding what it is they wish to know. By prompting students to take a more planful approach by first asking themselves what it is they want to know, a deeper understanding of mathematics is more likely. An amusing, if troubling, example (Reusser, 1987) of such mindlessness is provided by a group of first-grade and second-grade children, most of whom believed they had solved the following word problem, by manipulating the integers 26 and 10: "There are 26 sheep and 10 goats on a ship. How old is the captain?"

Using this sorry example as our illustration, a planful task-analysis approach can be rewarded directly by giving students additional points when they indicate their reasons for adding, subtracting, multiplying, or dividing, identify exactly what the problem is, or indicate what additional information is needed in order to solve the problem.

Curiosity Motive

The readiness of students to use their minds in productive ways depends on their willingness to go deeper into questions, to find problems everywhere, and to be puzzled by the obvious. Having low reading and writing skills is no barrier to this kind of challenge. Curiosity expresses itself in at least three ways, each of which can be honored in schools and rewarded directly as part of the equity game.

First, curiosity expresses itself as *question-asking*—inquiring, probing, and speculating. A questioning mind is central to all good problem-solving and sustains learning in various ways. Sometimes question-asking serves a fact-finding function (e.g., "What is that brown sediment at the bottom of the fish tank?"). Sometimes questions are used to determine what additional information is needed to solve a problem (e.g., "When was the fish tank last cleaned?"). At other times, questioning can frame possible answers or hypotheses (e.g., "Did the fish die for a lack of oxygen?").

Second, according to Albert Einstein, *problem-finding* is

the highest form of curiosity. Not that humans need look for more problems; problems seem to find us! Nonetheless, problem-finding is essential to human progress, often recognizing an unspoken need or anticipating a potential, but still unnoticed danger. In effect, problem-finding is looking for trouble that, if gone undetected, may multiply and put humans in harm's way.

A third manifestation of curiosity is a *sensitivity to mysterious, puzzling, and inconsistent facts or situations.* The ability to detect inconsistencies and puzzles in nature is the cornerstone of all science. For example, instead of simply getting rid of the bacteria killed by a green mold that spoiled his experiment, Alexander Fleming paused to consider the meaning of this accident, which led to the discovery of penicillin.

How can teachers arrange school assignments so that question-asking, problem-finding, and sensitivity can be systematically rewarded? Following are some examples reflecting each of the three aspects of curiosity mentioned above.

Question-asking

Asking questions about a topic stimulates curiosity and interest in learning more.

> **ACTIVITY 11** **African country report II:** Karen extended the African report described earlier to include a question-asking component. She requested that students list several questions about their country whose answers could not be found in any of the material they surveyed. Had Karen chosen to do so, she might have promoted question-asking skills further by having those students whose countries were geographic neighbors form into teams. These teams could then create questions about their common regions.

Problem Finding

Exercises in problem generation strengthen the view that every situation is a possible source of interesting problems and unasked questions.

| ACTIVITY 12 | **The Aswan High Dam:** Students are invited to make up arithmetic word problems |

The Aswan High Dam: Students are invited to make up arithmetic word problems based on facts provided by the teacher (using addition, subtraction, multiplication, and division for younger students and fractions or percentages for older students). These problems are then given to other students or teams of students to solve. Students receive points for each word problem successfully solved by others. Consider an example adapted from the *Productive Thinking Program* (Covington, Crutchfield, Davies, & Olton, 1974) and appropriate to the upper elementary and middle school levels:

> The Abu Simbel statues and temples were built some 3200 years ago by King Ramses II in Egypt. In 1960, when Egypt built the Aswan High Dam, the temples and statues would have been covered by the lake created behind the dam. The race was on to save these artifacts. The solution chosen was to cut the statues and temples into large pieces, and have each piece lifted to the top of the nearby mountain, where, far above the high-water mark, these ancient monuments would be put back together.

A sample of the kinds of facts students might use to create arithmetic word problems includes:

1. It took 25,000 slaves 20 years to build the temple. Outside Ramses' temple are 4 huge statues. Each statue is 67 feet high and weighs 12,000 tons. The heads of the statues are 15 feet high and each weighs 19 tons. Standing before a smaller temple are 6 smaller statues, each 33 feet high and weighing 700 tons; each head is 6 feet high and weighs 10 tons.

2. The work to save the temple and statues began on March 1, 1964, when the lake was only 35 feet below the temple. The water rose at the rate of one-half inch per day. Fifteen-hundred workers were divided into two groups of equal size. One group worked 12 hours during the day, the other 12 hours at night.

3. Each person worked 7 days a week and was paid 25 cents per hour. About 10,000 pounds of food were needed each day to feed the workers.

| ACTIVITY 13 | **African country report III:** Karen's African country report can be easily expanded to include a problem-generating element. Each regional team whose members represent neighboring countries could create arithmetic word problems for other teams to solve based on information about regional climate, exports and imports, or life expectancy statistics.

The more general technique of having students ask questions and formulate problems prior to their work on an assignment has many advantages. This technique helps organize material around important issues, fosters a sense of discovery and active participation in the act of learning, and tends to stimulate student interest. This technique is particularly useful in the teaching of elementary mathematics and in solving simple algebraic equations first encountered by middle school students. By working backwards, such as by inventing word problems rather than always solving them, students are forced to organize their thinking in entirely new ways. They must recognize the kinds of arithmetic operations implied by a problem and determine precisely what information is needed in order to solve it. Recall those hapless students who blithely solved the problem of the captain's age by using the number of sheep and goats on board his ship for their calculations. Had these students practiced inventing word problems of the kind suggested here, they probably would not have found themselves in such a "sheepish" position.

Discovering Mysteries, Puzzles, and Oddities

Nothing stimulates one's curiosity like a mystery. Teachers have always found that posing an assignment in terms of a puzzle is a sure winner. But instead of rewarding only the answer to the puzzle, teachers can also reinforce those skills associated with the discovery of the facts that make the problem a mystery in the first place (e.g., "I will give one point for each thing you write down about this mystery that seems odd or puzzling"). Such an exercise strengthens the willingness to notice and investigate facts that seem incongruous or surprising and, of course, to see the extraordinary in the ordinary. This kind of productive curiosity lies at the very heart of all scientific discovery and historical analysis.

ACTIVITY 14 | **The mystery of the *Mary Celeste*:** The *Mary Celeste* was a wooden sailing vessel whose most famous voyage started in early November, 1872. She sailed from New York carrying a cargo of 17,000 barrels of alcohol, which can be highly explosive. She was not seen until a month later, when she was sighted by another ship. Although under full sail, the *Mary Celeste* was weaving around in a strange way. Several sailors from the other ship boarded the *Mary Celeste* to investigate. What they found became the greatest sea mystery of all time. No one, either living or dead, was found on board. The *Mary Celeste* was sailing by herself!

Nothing was missing, except for the compass used to guide the ship and one lifeboat. Other than these missing items, the *Mary Celeste* was undamaged and the cargo untouched. In fact, everything was in its proper place. Even the sailors' boots were lined up in neat rows by their bunks, and in the captain's cabin there was an unfinished breakfast on the table.

Besides the obvious puzzle that no one was found on board the *Mary Celeste*, students can also be given credit for identifying these additional oddities: (a) the neat line of sailors' boots; (b) the unfinished breakfast; (c) the missing lifeboat; and (d) the missing compass.

Many experts believe that the key to everything was the cargo of alcohol. They believe that something made the captain and his crew think the cargo was about to explode, so they abandoned the ship quickly. But the cargo did not explode, and the Mary Celeste sailed on into history, leaving the captain and his crew without food or water to die hundreds of miles from land (adapted from the *Productive Thinking Program*; Covington, Crutchfield, Davies, & Olton, 1974).

STEP 3: REWARD MULTIPLE ABILITIES

We have argued that a preoccupation with one's ability undercuts the will to learn. This does not mean, however, that teachers should minimize the importance of ability or attempt to treat all students alike. The danger to learning is not that students differ in ability or even so much that they often judge their strengths and weaknesses in relative terms, compared with one another. Rather, the problem ultimately lies in the kinds of beliefs students hold about the nature of ability. When ability is viewed as a fixed, immutable capacity, students will likely despair if they judge themselves inadequate and they believe nothing can be done to restore the situation. By contrast, viewing ability as an expandable resource for solving problems that grows with knowledge and experience infuses students with a sense of optimism for future success. Optimism also depends on the view that ability is multidimensional with many forms, each of which is shared to one degree or another by all students.

> Schools typically encourage a narrow view of ability limited to verbal, logical, and abstract reasoning skills.

Unfortunately, schools typically encourage a narrow view of ability limited to verbal, logical, and abstract reasoning skills. However, the evidence suggests that there are many kinds of ability—many ways for youngsters not only to learn but also to demonstrate what they have learned. To the extent that schools disallow the expression of one's ideas by alternative means, they limit the ways in which youngsters can feel successful. Thus, for the same reasons we advocated extending the yardstick of success beyond the narrow view of winning over others to include success defined in terms of self-improvement and setting realistic goals, we now propose rewarding ideas and thoughts expressed through many modes of ability.

What are these multiple abilities? The best known list comes from the work of Howard Gardner (1993), who divided general intelligence into seven components of ability:

1. *Linguistic Ability:* The capacity to represent one's thoughts and ideas in words, either written or spoken.

2. *Logical-Mathematical Ability:* The ability to think in terms of numbers and quantitative relationships and to reason in a logical fashion.

3. *Spatial Ability:* The capacity to think in visual or spatial terms.

4. *Bodily-Kinesthetic Ability:* The ability to express one's ideas and feelings through gesture and bodily movement, and the possession of physical skills, including dexterity, coordination, and speed.

5. *Musical Ability:* The ability to think in musical forms, including a sensitivity to musical tones, rhythm, and pitch.

6. *Interpersonal Ability:* The capacity to detect various moods, intentions, and emotions in others, and to act on this information in order to influence groups and individuals.

7. *Intrapersonal Ability:* A sensitivity to one's own motives, feelings, and ways of thinking, as well as the ability to make realistic judgments about one's strengths and weaknesses for purposes of self-discovery and self-discipline.

Encouraging the use of as many of these kinds of abilities as possible is an important tool for enhancing the will to learn, in at least three ways. A multiple ability approach to classroom learning serves, first, to provide alternative forms of expression; second, to enrich existing strengths; and third, to provide the means for discovering hidden talents.

Alternative Expression

Students often master concepts, but are at a handicap for demonstrating their understanding if the only means to do so is limited to the verbal arena. By allowing students alternate forms of expression, say, by creating a diagram (spatial ability) or by pantomiming (bodily kinesthetic ability), students can demonstrate knowledge that otherwise might go unrecognized and hence unrewarded. This is not meant to imply that some students lack verbal and abstract reasoning capabilities altogether, but rather that these abilities for the moment are less developed for some students than others. Working to overcome one's limitations in one ability mode requires a long-term commitment and persistence, qualities of motivation that can be reinforced along the way by periodic successes in other ability modes.

Enrichment

Encouraging the expression of multiple abilities has an enriching function. This occurs when students are given the choice of demonstrating what they have learned in ways that are most comfortable for them through their most developed abilities. By allowing youngsters to draw on their strengths and talents, teachers accent the positive side of learning, that is, what one has achieved uniquely and is what one is especially capable of achieving. This kind of encouragement offsets the tendency of schools to assess students by probing for what they don't know or don't do very well. As has been noted, motivationally speaking, students learn with greater enthusiasm when they know that their grades will depend more on their successes than on their mistakes.

> Viewing ability as an expandable resource infuses students with a sense of optimism.

Exploration

Allowing expression of multiple abilities can also serve an exploratory function. By being encouraged to try different ways of conveying what one has learned through a variety of modes such as musical, kinesthetic, or spatial, students may discover hidden talents or new, attractive styles of organizing their knowledge. Discovering new sources of personal satisfaction and unique ways of expressing oneself, like having unexpected successes, is a continuing stimulant to learning.

These observations suggest several concrete ways that a multiple-ability approach can be introduced into classroom life as part of a larger effort to establish motivational equity—everyone striving for positive reasons open to all via multiple abilities.

| ACTIVITY 15 | **Tracking Sherlock Holmes:** Obviously, verbal and linguistic skills are key to the future occupational success of virtually every student in ways |

that musical or kinesthetic abilities are not likely to be. Everyone must learn to read with comprehension and write with clarity, and these priorities must form the centerpiece of any efforts at school reform. How, then, can we reconcile these linguistic priorities with multiple-ability expression? Fortunately, assignments can be arranged so that both goals can be served simultaneously.

For example, students can demonstrate their comprehension of a written passage (linguistic/reading) in any one of several other modes of ability using an approach suggested by Thomas Armstrong (1994). Students might be assigned to read a passage from Sir Arthur Conan Doyle's story, *A Study in Scarlet*, in which he describes the personality and unique worldviews of Sherlock Holmes. Then, rather than giving a multiple-choice test in which students might be required to choose the single best description of Sherlock Holmes, the teacher allows students to demonstrate their understanding of Sherlock Holmes in any one of the following ways:

■ *Linguistic Presentation:* Describe Sherlock Holmes in your own words, either orally or in a brief essay.

■ *Logical-Mathematical Presentation:* Describe the way Sherlock Holmes' mind works as a kind of logic machine.

■ *Spatial Presentation:* Draw a picture of Sherlock Holmes' face with an expression you believe best characterizes him.

■ *Bodily-Kinesthetic Presentation:* Pantomime the body posture and facial expression that you feel best expresses Sherlock Holmes's personality.

- *Musical Presentation:* What popular song or music best describes Holmes? Explain why.

- *Interpersonal Presentation:* What real-life individual reminds you of Sherlock Holmes? Explain why.

- *Intrapersonal Presentation:* If you were Sherlock Holmes, what would be your feelings in the situation described in the story?

| ACTIVITY 16 | **Teaching Bernoulli's Principle:** A variation on the previous example illustrates how |

a multiple-ability approach applies to teaching concepts as well as to expressing what one has learned. Consider teaching Bernoulli's principle to high school students. The students are first presented with Bernoulli's principle in a verbal form (linguistic mode): "The speed of airflow is greater over the curved top surface of an aircraft wing compared to the speed across the flat undersurface, thereby causing upward pressure under the wing."

To insure a fuller understanding of the concept and of the larger metaphorical uses for terms like *pressure*, students might be asked to create a visual image of the principle by imagining a flag flying straight out in a high wind (visual). A bodily-kinesthetic counterpart of Bernoulli's principle might involve having students hold a sheet of paper in front of them and blow gently over the top surface, causing the paper to rise. In another variation, students might imagine themselves becoming molecules of air moving greater distances across the top of the wing than the bottom. Finally, a metaphorical extension of "being under pressure" can be explored by asking students to recall those times in their lives when they were "under pressure" and whether they felt they had a great deal or very little psychological space (intrapersonal).

| ACTIVITY 17 | **African country report IV:** School assignments can also be arranged so that any or all |

of the three goals of the multiple-ability approach can be served within the same task. For example, in an innovative extension of the African country report, Karen might have assigned students the task of creating a travel packet for potential visitors to their country. Students could draw up an itinerary for visitors with an accompanying time line (spatial); design a series of tickets for entry to various historic sites (visual/spatial); create and carry out various dance steps as part of a potential advertising video (bodily-kinesthetic); or compile a list of useful phrases and questions in the native language for tourists (linguistic).

Whenever projects are structured around several work options, as in this example, students can be given a choice of which option to complete, or they might be required to complete all the options. In this latter case, students might be allowed to decide which of the completed options would be graded pass/fail and which would be assigned either a letter grade or points.

Once again, the strategy behind allowing student choice concerns maximizing the chances that students will be evaluated in ways (modes) that they find most comfortable. Alternately, an exploratory function is favored when students are required to complete all aspects of the assignment, thereby gaining some familiarity in working across several ability modes.

| ACTIVITY 18 | **A multiple-abilities questionnaire:** Before Karen allows her students to choose from a variety of assignments featuring different kinds of abilities, she asks them to fill out the following questionnaire. As one can see in Exhibit D, the questionnaire directs students to indicate how they judge their abilities in each of a number of areas. In this way, Karen hopes the students will broaden their definition of ability. |

NAME _____

DATE _____

Multiple-Talents/Abilities Questionnaire

DIRECTIONS: PUT AN "X" IN THE COLUMN UNDER THE BEST DESCRIPTION OF YOUR TALENT AND/OR ABILITY IN EACH OF THE AREAS ON THE LEFT:

ABILITIES	STRONG	AVERAGE	WEAK
READING			
WRITING			
DRAWING			
SPEAKING (ORAL REPORTS, SKITS, DISCUSSIONS, ETC.)			
ACTING			
DIRECTING			
SINGING			
RHYTHM (DANCING)			
GROUP LEADER			
SPATIAL RELATIONS (MAP READING, DOING PUZZLES, ETC.)			

ACTIVITY 19 **A multiple-abilities checklist:** Providing students with the following checklist may help them think of alternative ways to express their understanding of subject-matter concepts in any field using different ability modalities.

■ Invent a game to illustrate an idea

■ Do an experiment

■ Make a journal

■ Create a time line

■ Make a map

- Debate an idea with opposing views

- Make a model or replica

- Write a lyric for a song

- Do a radio script

- Take pictures with a camera or camcorder

- Draw a mural or poster

- Make a chart with numbers

- Think up an advertisement to sell an idea or concept

- Make a drawing and cut it into pieces of a puzzle

- Make up a dance step

- Conduct an interview

- Write a project report

- Make a scrapbook

STEP 4: OFFER ALTERNATIVE INCENTIVES

Having considered ways to reward intrinsic reasons for learning through multiple abilities, is anything more needed? Yes. At this point, readers might consider the nature of rewards themselves and another source of equity—that is, providing rewards of equal incentive value for all students.

Meaningful Rewards

For rewards to sustain learning, they must be valued by the learner. Many youngsters may not realize the long-term benefits of good grades. Even the definition of a *good grade* varies among them (Teel, 1995). To these students, grades as a medium of exchange are meaningless. Some students are indifferent to the prospects of receiving report cards, quarterly progress reports, or other official evidence of their progress or lack of it. Sometimes such indifference reflects the belief that grades are irrelevant to survival in one's world.

In any event, if rewards—be they grades or gold stars—hold no attraction or, worse yet, are irrelevant, they will be ignored, and as a result, the target behaviors they are intended to strengthen will suffer. From this perspective, then, teachers need to identify those incentives valued by youngsters. It is our hope, of course, that grades and grading will eventually become a positive motivating factor in the minds of all youngsters. But for this to happen, teachers must forge a new meaning for grades in which they are no longer perceived by children as bribes for compliance. Grades must come to serve as a valued source of feedback whose purpose it is to promote intrinsic goals, that is, grades as information about how well one is doing, how one can improve, and how much is left to do. In addition, teachers must convince students of the long-term importance of good grades (e.g., college, careers). Meanwhile, until grades and grading are seen in a positive light by more youngsters, other kinds of rewards may be needed to sustain learning.

Table 1 displays several categories of tangible incentives most frequently employed by teachers.

TABLE 1
CATEGORIES OF TANGIBLE INCENTIVES

Edible	_School Prizes_	_Privileges_	_Social Recognition_
gum	paper	choosing stories	praise
candy	crayons	paper monitor	good grades
ice cream	notepads	free time	certificates
cookies	pencils	computer time	gold stars
cupcakes	bookmarkers	library time	being correct
			getting a problem right

Naturally, these categories are not mutually exclusive. For example, getting a problem right (social recognition) can never be completely separated from the privileges that success commands. Nonetheless, for our purposes, these distinctions are useful because they simplify an otherwise highly complex notion.

At the elementary school level, most teachers make use of one or more of the reinforcers from each of the categories. Younger children prefer more tangible rewards, especially food, whereas older students prefer social reinforcers in the form of recognition and praise. These findings do not imply a perfect match between the rewards offered by teachers on a blanket basis and student preferences. Far from it. When it comes to teachers predicting what specific rewards are preferred by most children, the record is surprisingly poor. In one study (Daly, Jacob, King, & Cheramine, 1984), fifth- and sixth-grade teachers predicted the two school-related reinforcers they believed students would prefer most—"When your teacher buys materials that you especially like," and "Getting the right answer." Of these two reinforcers, only "Getting the right answer" was also ranked high by children, and then only among girls. Obviously, it is important to consider gender differences as well as other differences, such as the child's age, interests, and emotional development, when gauging student preferences for rewards.

Another factor also complicates teachers' predictions. Student preferences also depend on the circumstances under which learning takes place. For example, preschool children prefer social reinforcers if the assignment is done on a one-to-one basis with the teacher (Daly et al., 1984). These same students prefer tangible reinforcers for the identical assignment if it is done with a group of children. Little wonder that observers have concluded that many of the reinforcers listed in Table 1 are "floaters," that is, their reward value differs for the same student from time to time and task to task, and even differs depending on a childs' place in the learning process.

> Students themselves should be involved in the process of identifying potentially valued reinforcers.

All this suggests that when implementing a tangible reward structure of any kind, students themselves should be involved in the process of identifying potentially valued reinforcers.

Turning Work Back into Play

Using tangible rewards to promote learning recalls a fundamental concern raised earlier. Recall the evidence indicating that when students are offered tangible rewards for what they would otherwise do spontaneously, play is turned into work. Recall also that work is something people are paid to do, so students stop learning when rewards are withdrawn. Actually, offering extrinsic incentives need not interfere with the willingness to learn, depending on several factors within the control of teachers.

First, giving rewards for participation alone is less likely to inhibit intrinsic involvement than if the rewards are given in an effort to control the quality of the student's work (Deci & Ryan, 1985). In the former case, rewards offered simply for trying function only as an invitation to perform, and are less likely to carry with them feelings of being controlled or of being under the threat of censorship, thereby freeing students to respond in more intrinsically engaging ways. Incidentally, *contingency contracting* is an ideal vehicle for taking advantage of this fact. In this case the offering or withholding of a reward depends totally on the individual's decision to participate or not, and it is up to the student to negotiate the prevailing standards of excellence.

> For rewards to sustain learning, they must be valued by the learner.

Second, when students have a choice of rewards, the sense of being controlled or being under surveillance is reduced. Likewise, being able to control the rewards, as in the case of rewarding oneself for setting realistic goals—recall the example of the spelling bee (Activity 4)—makes rewards even less intrusive. One possibility for extending the degree to which students control the available rewards involves allowing them to choose the particular assignment on which they will be graded. Or, as was suggested in an earlier section, allow students the choice of how much each of several assignments or tests will count toward their final grade.

Third, when grades are awarded on an absolute basis, they tend to serve an informational, not an arousal, function. Grades or points become meaningful because they indicate completion of a specific accomplishment. Once again, when grades provide feedback rather than being mainly a means to motivate the student, intrinsic goals are more adequately served (Butler & Nisan, 1986).

Fourth, the negative effects of tangible rewards on intrinsic engagement can be minimized to the extent that these incentives are used sparingly, and only as absolutely needed. This concept, known as the principle of *minimal sufficiency*, suggests that rewards need to be removed or reduced in amount or frequency as soon as the skills to be learned are adequately established.

With safeguards like these in place, the evidence is that once students begin mastering a topic or a course of study, and thereby experience an increasing sense of progress or improvement, a natural shift occurs spontaneously, with students' performances coming more and more under intrinsic control. The classic example of this process is provided by two researchers, Harold Cohen and James Filipczak (1971), who worked with delinquent boys. A so-called *token economy* was established in which the boys were paid in the form of tokens for satisfactorily completing homework assignments in mathematics and reading. The tokens quickly took on value for the boys, in the same way that money does, not because money or tokens have any intrinsic appeal, but because of what they can buy. For these boys, the tokens could be exchanged for various privileges of the kind listed in Table 1. In the beginning, tangible prizes and privileges unrelated to the act of learning were most sought after by the boys. But as their achievement test scores improved, reflecting greater mastery of content, a marked change occurred in how the boys spent their tokens. They began to purchase library time and pay rent on individual study cubicles. In effect, learning itself had become a sought-after goal. Other researchers have also reported the same kinds of transformation (e.g., Allen, 1975). This system is reminiscent of the grading sys-

> Once students begin mastering a topic and experience an increasing sense of improvement, a natural shift occurs spontaneously, with students' performances coming more and more under intrinsic control.

tem employed in Karen's classroom, except that tokens were replaced by grade points.

ACTIVITY 20 **A token economy:** One of the most important implications of Step 4 is that reward structures in classrooms should remain flexible and individualized. To be most effective, in theory, then, not all children should receive the same incentives at the same time. However, for obvious logistical reasons, such individualization may not be possible. It may simply be too much for the teacher to monitor. One practical solution is to set up a token economy of the kind featured in the research by Cohen and Filipczak. Essentially, as students accumulate points for various amounts and quality of work, these points can be credited toward privileges or prizes of the child's own choosing. Token economies promote equal reinforcement for different individuals who may have different preferences—another kind of equity—all accomplished through the individual choices of students with a minimum of teacher involvement.

ACTIVITY 21 **The Premack principle:** A variation on the token economy concept simplifies things even more by eliminating the need for teachers to provide actual prizes. It involves the application of the *Premack principle*. In this case, the teacher uses a behavior preferred by the student to reinforce an intrinsically less interesting behavior. Behavioral jargon aside, this simply means that students are given an opportunity to complete one task so that they may do another that is more pleasurable to them (e.g., "First, complete these 10 math problems, then you may read the next chapter in the Star Trek adventure"). No tokens are necessary in this kind of exchange, and again it is the student, not the teacher, who tailors the reward to fit his or her current interest. There is also the added advantage that these self-rewards may directly promote the goals of learning, as in the example of the Star Trek adventure, where improved reading comprehension is a likely and valued outcome.

ACTIVITY 22 **Nonschool rewards:** Teachers generally overestimate the reward value of school-related incentives for students, such as grades, teacher praise, and classroom privileges. Conversely, teachers underestimate the intrinsic value of nonschool-related rewards. For example, in one study, both boys and girls rated as their number one choice of rewards, "Going to a different, faraway place on vacation" (Daly et al., 1984). Although this particular wish is likely to remain a wish, teachers should not neglect the potential sources of rewards outside of school. Moreover, when possible, parents can be enlisted to help both select and administer those incentives for learning.

STEP 5: MAKE ASSIGNMENTS ENGAGING

A final source of equity depends on the curriculum. The job of encouraging positive reasons for learning should not be left solely to the way teachers arrange classroom rewards. School assignments themselves should invite personal growth, foster creative expression, and engender discovery and inquiry for all students. First, when a task has the power to elicit creative thinking, the use of tangible incentives to reward participation can be removed that much sooner. Second, when students are intrinsically engaged, grades and grading are seen in a more positive light—as a form of guidance and information, rather than something conveying the threat of punishment. Third, students are more willing to take intellectual risks when they are in the thrall of an engaging task, despite the presence of grades and grading (Covington & Wiedenhaupt, 1996).

Naturally, not all assignments can be fully engaging, and teachers need not always try to make them so. After all, teachers are not in the entertainment business. Students must realize that sometimes learning is tedious and unglamorous and can be a chore. Nonetheless, things go best, motivationally speaking, whenever school assignments promote motivational equity—that is, when all students can strive for positive reasons. When students can express feelings of resolve, share in the satisfaction that comes from knowing they have done the best they can, and know that they have succeeded in their own way, education is most satisfying.

What are the characteristics of tasks that permit such

intrinsic engagement? First, assignments are inherently attractive to the extent that they are *novel* and *intriguing*. Second, tasks are inherently engaging to the extent that they further the student's own personal *interests*. Third, assignments are inherently appealing to the extent that they are *relevant*—relevant to the student's own history and to his or her search for personal identity, relevant to the real, pressing issues facing society, and relevant to the student's future.

Making Tasks Novel

Novel not only means "out of the ordinary," but sometimes means "out of this world" also. Assignments are captivating to the degree that they stimulate the kinds of fanciful thinking involved in creating imaginary worlds that is so crucial to social and scientific progress. These skills involve the capacity to imagine the impossible as potentially possible. It was these qualities of mind that led Christopher Cockrell to invent the hovercraft when he played with the unlikely possibility of moving ships over the water, not through it.

Another characteristic of free, unfettered thought is referred to as *divergent thinking*. Divergent thinking involves searching for ideas, speculating, and going off in different directions, sometimes playfully, even mischievously, while suspending assumptions about present realities and exploring unlikely but not illogical possibilities. Divergent thinking has often been associated with the tendency to be open to experience and with *creativity*—another kind of ability shared to one degree or another by everyone.

| ACTIVITY 23 | **Divergent thinking:** Divergent thinking is important in evaluating ideas and plans or proposals for action. Often the appropriateness of an idea depends more on the future consequences of putting it to work than on its immediate intended impact.

The Aswan Dam project (see page 74) provides an excellent example of humankind's inability to anticipate the kinds of problems and difficulties that may arise as a consequence of modifying natural processes. According to experts, the building of this dam has led to severe erosion of the Nile River basin, a breakdown of the aquatic food chain in the Eastern Mediterranean, a rising salt level that threatens to sterilize the rich Nile soil, and the aggravation of various public health problems. A concise, nontechnical report of this situation is found in "Aswan Dam Looses a Flood of Problems," by Claire Sterling (*Life*, February 12, 1971).

As an extension of the African country report, teachers can invite students whose countries include or border on the Nile basin to demonstrate their prowess in divergent thinking by speculating on all the possible positive and negative consequences of damming up the Nile River ("I will give one point for each idea suggested toward your grade on the African reports").

ACTIVITY 24 **Understanding failure:** In this activity students can discover, belatedly, the failures of others to anticipate problems caused by their own actions. Although no one wants to experience failure, we are all nonetheless fascinated by failure and its consequences. Teachers can take advantage of this fact to make several important observations about the true nature of failure, or as Max Beerbohm remarked, "There is much to be said for failure. It is more interesting than success." The first lesson is that making mistakes is an important part of all problem-solving. In fact, successful thinkers actually make more mistakes than those who give up easily. The second lesson is that most mistakes can be set right by trying again with the guidance of hindsight.

Teachers may wish to reinforce their students' understanding of the indispensable role of mistakes in learning by replaying some of history's most famous failures. For example, a high school civics teacher might give credit to her students for each flaw they uncover in the reasoning that led the American leadership to embark on the disastrous Bay of Pigs invasion of Cuba in the early 1960's, and provide additional rewards for proposing ways to correct the political decision-making process so that minority views will be taken more seriously.[1] Another, more humorous approach to the same topic is found in James Welles's fascinating book, *The Story of Stupidity: A History of Western Idiocy from the Days of Greece to the Moment You Saw this Book*.[2]

Enlisting Student Interest

Arranging school assignments around student interests is a powerful motivational tool. Being personally involved in a task stimulates intrinsic engagement. Equally important, intrinsically engaged students perceive the purpose of grades in positive ways (Covington & Wiedenhaupt, 1996). When interest in an assignment is high, students believe that grades actually inspire them to do their best. The reactions to grades are quite different when these same students work on tasks that hold little personal interest. In this instance, they perceive grades as being used by teachers to force them to do at least a minimum job. Not surprisingly, when student interest is low or nonexistent, intrinsic reasons for achievement suffer, leaving only artificially induced incentives like the threat of a bad grade or the anticipation of a good grade as the main source of motivation. When

> School assignments should invite personal growth and creative expression.

grades drive achievement, they are often seen by students not as a measure of the quality of their work, but as a measure of their worth as well. These beliefs lead disinterested students to worry about grades as they work, to feel incompetent, or to complain that they did not get enough grade credit for the amount of work required.

Obviously, it is to everyone's advantage to arrange school tasks around student interests when possible. But what can teachers do to motivate students when assignments are essentially chores to be completed—unglamorous or even boring, with little hope for relating them to student interests? The learning of facts such as the state capitals, or the memorizing of glossary terms or symbols such as the table of periodic elements, falls in the category

[1]For a description of the Bay of Pigs disaster and other planning failures, see Hall, P. (1980). *Great planning disasters*. Berkeley, CA: University of California Press.
[2]See Welles, J. (1988). *The story of Stupidity: A history of Western idiocy from the days of Greece to the moment you saw this book*. Orient, NY: Mount Pleasant Press.

of chores. Fortunately, these chores can be transformed into meaningful work by making the facts to be learned relevant to other assignments of greater interest. This can be accomplished in several ways.

First, students can learn factual information *in advance* of its use in solving a problem. This arrangement is consistent with the mastery learning paradigm (see page 60–63), in which students are required to learn material to the level of some predetermined criteria using several study/test sessions, if needed, before they are allowed to proceed. For example, a teacher who wishes to prepare a unit on safety in the workplace might use the disaster at the Chernobyl nuclear plant in Ukraine as a prime example of bad equipment design and poor training of the operating staff. Students are allowed to replay the Chernobyl disaster (in simulated form), with classmates taking on the role of key, Soviet personnel, but only after everyone learns various facts and principles about occupational safety that are relevant to this drama. Here the opportunity to participate in an intriguing role-playing task is contingent on students first mastering certain basic facts and ground rules. This is another example of the Premack Principle (page 89).

Second, facts can also be introduced *during* problem solving, when students in the previous example are trying desperately to figure out how to shut down the Chernobyl reactor before it goes critical. In this example, the teacher might call time-out and give players the remainder of the class period to study information that might assist them in making the best decisions. What better way to convince students of the value of having the right information at the right time?

Third, facts can be introduced *after* a problem-solving episode is completed as a kind of postmortem review. For instance, students might identify those facts from a list provided by the teacher that, had it been available sooner, might have helped prevent a nuclear meltdown.

| ACTIVITY 25 | **Rote learning revitalized:**   Basically, these three teaching strategies serve as object lessons, not just creative ways to conquer boredom and revitalize rote learning. More specifically, they illustrate the importance of facts—dull, lifeless, and routine as they may |

often appear. These strategies also aid students in seeing a larger purpose for facts, beyond being only things to think *about*—and then perhaps duly filed away—but facts also as things to think *with*.

| ACTIVITY 26 | **Making boring tasks interesting:** Teachers need not carry the entire burden of making learning relevant and interesting. Students should share much of this responsibility, and in the process they can learn a valuable skill, that of turning boring tasks into interesting ones. The will to learn and to continue learning is well served when the tedious aspects of learning can be made interesting. The classic example involves the hapless employee whose job it was to inspect potato chips for uniformity of appearance, and who, in the midst of this mindless activity, seized on the strategy which made everything more tolerable: looking for meaningful shapes, such as the image of Elvis Presley, in the nonuniform chips (Sansone, Weir, Harpster, & Morgan, 1992).

When students next face repetitive chores, the burden will be lighter if they are first given an opportunity in groups to discuss ways to make the best of the situation.

Making Tasks Relevant

Relevancy has many meanings, but in all its forms, relevancy is a powerful inducement to learning. Consider the notion of personal relevance.

| ACTIVITY 27 | **Assignments relevant to one's past: African country report V:** There are few reasons as personally compelling as being able to place oneself in a historical context, as the member of a group defined by ethnic heritage, by family ties, by region, or by nationality. As an addendum to the African country report, Karen might have asked those of her students who are of African descent to research their family histories by interviewing parents and grandparents in an effort to locate the

region where their descendants originated. Students of other ethnic backgrounds could work on their own family-origin reports.

ACTIVITY 28 | **Assignments of real-world relevance:** Perhaps the supreme source of motivation and personal relevance for all learners is being respected enough for one's ideas that others seek out our advice. One of the best ways to engage students in the role of a surrogate expert whose advice and ideas are valued is the use of simulations, or so-called *serious games* (Abt, 1987)—serious in that they reflect real issues. Serious games are not games of mere amusement or frivolous diversion, but are games that reflect the most potential economic, political, and social problems confronting our society. They can be viewed as games or contests, often played by adversaries with unequal resources, including knowledge, skills, and power. Sometimes adversaries are not other people, but conditions that threaten the entire community, like the problem of worldwide hunger and other problems that can be eliminated only when players cooperate in a common cause.

The motivational benefits of simulations and role playing are many. For one thing, games are natural vehicles for engendering a cooperative spirit. For another thing, serious games are also well suited to demonstrating the functional value of knowledge. Classrooms need not be seen as the purveyors of irrelevant or useless information, cut off from the realities of daily living. Simulations can also transform the teacher–student relationship for the better. Here the teacher becomes the natural ally of the players—helping, coaching, providing information as requested, and sometimes even becoming a player. The adversary is no longer an adult authority figure who dictates rules and enforces them. This function is now taken over by the rules and restrictions of the game itself. Indeed, even the rebellious student, fearing rejection by one's fellow players, is more likely to play by peer group rules than by the rules imposed by a teacher.

1 What strategies or teaching methods are you already using that are compatible with an equity game?

2 Is there anything about the equity game as we portray it that you find contrary to your present teaching methods?

3 If you would like to move more in the direction of an equity game, what changes, large or small, would you make in your own classroom?

SUMMARY

In this section we have considered various concrete ways to transform schooling from an ability to an equity game. Such changes generally take place slowly and typically only after protracted effort on the part of teachers, a process requiring patience and flexibility. Fortunately, even small changes initiated early on can make substantial changes down the line in terms of student motivation and achievement, as well as teacher morale. We next turn to some of the issues and obstacles that will confront teachers in the process of such a transformation.

SUGGESTED READINGS

Much of what we have advocated so far under Goal 2 is consistent with a mastery or student-based approach to learning. This approach requires that learning objectives be couched in absolute terms, with a specification of the particular standards by which students will be judged. Students are then given ample opportunity through repeated practice to improve and eventually to equal or surpass these standards. The following references provide a more detailed look at the application of such mastery principles in school settings:

Block, J. H. (1984). Making school learning activities more play-like: Flow and mastery learning. *The Elementary School Journal, 85*, 65–75.

Mitchell, D., & Spady, W. (1978). Organizational context for implementing outcome-based education. *Educational Researcher, 7*, 9–17.

Spady, W. G. (1982). Outcome-based instructional management: A sociological perspective. *The Australian Journal of Education, 26*, 123–143.

Many of the teaching suggestions in Goal 2 depend on the ability of students to set meaningful goals and to make realistic plans of action. The following references expand on the educational implications of each of the main themes.

Goal-setting

de Charms, R. (1957). Affiliation motive and productivity in small groups. *Journal of Abnormal and Social Psychology*, *55*, 222–226.

Diggory, J. C. (1966). *Self-evaluation: Concepts and studies.* New York: Wiley.

Locke, E. A. (1968). Toward a theory of task motivation and incentives. *Organizational Behavior and Human Performance*, *3*, 157–189.

Locke, E. A., & Latham, G. P. (1984). *Goal-setting: A motivational technique that works!* Englewood Cliffs, NJ: Prentice–Hall.

Planning

Covington, M. V. (1986). Instruction and problem solving in planning. In S. L. Friedman, E. K. Skolnick, and R. R. Cocking (Eds.), *Blueprints for thinking: The role of planning in cognitive development*, pp. 469–511. New York: Cambridge University Press.

Friedman, E. K., Skolnick, E. K., and Cocking, R. R. (1986). *Blueprints for thinking: The role of planning in cognitive development.* New York: Cambridge University Press.

In recent years, the multiple-ability approach to teaching (see Step 3, pages 77–84) has gained greatly in popularity. Following is a representative list of references describing both the theory behind this approach and its various practical applications.

Armstrong, T. (1993). *7 kinds of smart: Discovering and using your natural intelligences.* New York: Plume/Penguin.

Gardner, H. (1993). *Multiple intelligences: The theory and practice*. New York: Basic Books.

Gardner, H., & Hatch, T. (1989). Multiple intelligences go to school. *Educational Researcher, 18*(8) 4–10.

Lazear, D. (1991). *Seven ways of teaching: The artistry of teaching with multiple intelligences*. Palatine, IL: Skylight.

Teele, S. (1991). *Teaching and Assessment Strategies Appropriate for Multiple Intelligences*. Riverside, CA: University of California Extension (H101 Bannockburn, University of California, Riverside, CA 92521-0112).

Everyone loves a mystery! By their very nature, mysteries are the quintessential example of novelty, incorporating elements of the unknown, the unexplained, and the unexpected. The following references should prove helpful for suggesting ways in which different subject-matter content, ranging from history and science to English, can be cast in the form of real-life mystery problems to be solved (see Step 2, page 75).

Gould, R. T. (1965). *Enigmas: Another book of unexplained facts*. New York: University Books.

Gould, R. T. (1965). *Oddities: A book of unexplained facts*. New York: Allen & Co.

Hawkins, G. S. (1965). *Stonehenge decoded*. Garden City, NJ: Doubleday.

Heyerdahl, T. (1989). *Easter Island: The mystery solved*. New York: Random House.

Roueche, B. (1954). *Eleven blue men and other narratives of medical detection*. New York: Little, Brown & Co.

Serling, R. J. (1963). *The* Electra *story: The dramatic history of aviation's most controversial airliner*. New York: Doubleday.

Snow, E. R. (1967). *Incredible mysteries and legends of the sea*. New York: Dodd, Mead & Co.

Serious games (see Activity 28, page 96) have gained widespread acceptance in schools, especially with the advent of microcomputers beginning in the early 1980's (for an annotated review of available games, see Cruikshank, Telfer, Ezell, & Manford, 1987). Today hundreds of simulation games are commercially available. One need only consult the Yellow Pages for a local distributor or game store.

For those teachers interested in reviewing research on simulations and the theoretical bases for their use, the following references are useful:

Covington, M. V. (1992). *Making the grade: A self-worth perspective on motivation and school reform*. New York: Cambridge University Press.

Malone, T. W. (1981). Toward a theory of intrinsically motivating instruction. *Cognitive Science, 4*, 333–369.

Woodward, J., Carnie, D., & Gersten, R. (1988). Teaching problem solving through computer simulations. *American Educational Research Journal, 25*(1) 72–86.

goal 3

Overcoming Obstacles to Change

We do not want to leave the impression that the transition from an ability game to an equity game is necessarily smooth or easy. Furthermore, the transition is not trouble free for all students. There are several important obstacles to be reckoned with in the process of change.

STUDENT UNRESPONSIVENESS

Not all students respond well to change. Although we believe that establishing motivational equity is a necessary step in cultivating the will to learn, it is not always sufficient to turn things around. This is especially true for those youngsters, like Lydia from Ms. Jackson's class, who have come to accept failure as a way of life and blame their poor academic record on insufficient ability. Such youngsters are unlikely to take immediate advantage of the plentiful rewards available in an equity game. At first, they are likely to reject their successes by attributing them to chance, a lucky break, or a manufactured gesture by the teacher. This happens because success implies an obligation to do better the next time, something that these youngsters doubt they can do (Mettee, 1971). As a result, Lydia, and many students like her, are left with few achievements in school for which they can feel personally responsible and justly proud. But this is precisely what students with low expectations need. It is only when students struggle to succeed through hard work and persistence that they will be able to internalize the pride that accompanies such achievements, and thereby begin to rebuild a sense of personal worth and self-confidence.

Sometimes it may be necessary for teachers to arrange for such successes by literally insisting that reluctant students complete a project or an assignment satisfactorily. This may require mobilizing a full range of resources, including the soliciting of parents or guardians to help monitor a child's progress or requesting that students redo a report or essay until it meets minimally acceptable standards. Although this enforced process is often met initially with resistance by students, our research experience has been that in the end it pays dividends in terms of increased student enthusiasm and a willingness to work more diligently on subsequent school assignments.

> Success implies an obligation to do better the next time.

Teachers may ask, what of the tendency of these students not to accept their successes? To combat this tendency, the process of holding students to high standards of work must be made safe. It has been suggested that success threatens students because they believe it cannot be reproduced. However, if students are allowed to bring their achievements under their own control through a combination of proper task analysis, rewards for improvement, and realistic goal-setting, then success will be seen as repeatable.

INSUFFICIENT SKILLS

Many students are simply unprepared to take advantage of the independence and autonomy implied by an equity focus. Students may lack the time management skills needed to complete work contracts successfully, or they may not know how to correct their mistakes even when given an opportunity to do so. There are also failure-prone students who need independence and autonomy the most, but of all students, are the least able to manage their own learning. For many of these students, success is an unexpected event that they are unable to accept, let alone plan for. Moreover, they often deliberately misjudge their capacities and set irrational goals in an effort to protect a sense of worth.

Fortunately, the accumulated research of other investigators and our own experiences (Covington, 1986) suggest that a lack of planning skills as well as self-handicapping tendencies can be overcome through systematic skill training in ways that help students take responsibility for their own learning. This is not easy, however. In the beginning, some children will be confused by the freedom permitted them under an equity system, while others will pursue their own agendas in essentially undisciplined ways. Obviously, great patience needs to be exercised by the teacher. This virtue may be best served by remembering that encouraging an equity focus means more than simply changing the rules of the learning game; equally importantly, it requires assisting students in learning the skills needed to play by these new rules. From this perspective, many of the classroom exercises described in this book—especially those dealing with planfulness and goal-setting—are the skill

> The success of an equity focus depends on encouraging the underlying skills of originality, independence of thought, and autonomy.

components of the motivation to learn. These skills need practice in their own right.

In the long run, the success of an equity focus depends on encouraging the underlying skills of originality, independence of thought, and autonomy that sustain an equity focus. In turn, the exercise of these skills depends on the opportunity to use them and on being rewarded systematically for their application.

UNLIMITED REWARDS

Rewarding intrinsic reasons for learning poses several serious issues. Earlier, we addressed the possibility that by rewarding already intrinsically engaging activities, teachers may run the risk of turning play into work. We argued that this was a problem only in an ability game, and that by shifting to an equity game, rewards actually facilitate learning, not inhibit it.

Another problem not yet fully discussed stems from the fact that the rewards for being intrinsically engaged are essentially unlimited in number because they reside in the process of learning itself, as when the reward for satisfying one's curiosity is the knowledge gained. Anyone can be curious, and the potential rewards are limited only by the actions of the individual.

However, are not rewards devalued when they become too plentiful? Yes, in an ability game. The greater the number of students who do well, the more likely it is that the successes of the many will be attributed to an easy task because less able students, it is reasoned, can succeed only at something simple; conversely, the fewer who do well, the more success is attributed to high ability. In effect, the value of good grades in an ability game depends on their scarcity. However, in an equity game in which many students do well, success is counted in terms of hard work or of making significant progress—something everyone can do, but that is not necessarily attributable to an easy task or easy grading.

This transformation is precisely what occurred in Karen's experimental class. Recall that more and more of her students got higher and higher grades as the year progressed. At the same time, her students came to recognize that success was being measured in terms of improvement and progress even though the absolute criteria remained high. This meant that easier assignments were an unlikely explanation for improved grades. In fact, more often than not, students attributed their improved grades to an increased sense of self-confidence in their ability to do well and to a social climate for learning in

> Good grades remain meaningful, despite their frequency, as long as they are earned through hard work.

which all students were perceived as wanting to do better. When students remarked that the course was becoming easier, typically they believed not that the requirements were being reduced, but that their skill level was increasing. The point is that good grades remain meaningful, despite their frequency, as long as they are earned through hard work or improvement, qualities that imply that a task was difficult, not easy.

THE MYTHS OF COMPETITION

We have advised downplaying competition as a way to motivate students. As a motivator, competition destroys the will to learn. The evidence on this point is quite clear. Moreover, there is little support for the notion of *healthy competition*, that is, introducing competition in modest amounts. Any amount of competition, even carefully administered in small doses, produces a discernible decrease in learning. This is because whenever students are busy avoiding the feelings of failure, or attempting to make others fail, there is little room for true involvement in learning.

> In an equity game, success is counted in terms of hard work or significant progress.

Granting that competition is a dubious way to arouse learners, is it not important, some might ask, to introduce competition in schools in order to prepare students for the rigors of economic survival later on? To downplay competition, some might argue, is to prepare children for a world that does not exist. And does not competition also build character and fortitude? Faced with such arguments, many teachers may question the wisdom of deemphasizing a competitive ethos. These are powerful claims in favor of competition that must be rebutted before an equity approach can be fully justified.

First, the claim that competition (or adversity) builds character is flatly contradicted by the evidence (for a review, see Kohn, 1986). In their efforts to avoid losing (in the ability game), students learn to lie, cheat, and become saboteurs, not only of others, but of themselves as well, when they adopt failure-avoiding strategies that, ironically, guarantee the very failures they are attempting to avoid. Far from building character, then, competition in schools contributes to a breakdown in personal integrity.

Competition destroys the will to learn.

Second, what of the argument that competition in schools prepares students for survival in the outside world? The essential paradox facing those who make this argument is that forcing students to compete in school actually undercuts their capacity to compete in any kind of world, competitive or not. Competition prompts the loss of self-confidence, increases resentment, and makes for timid, indecisive, and self-doubting individuals. This is no proper legacy with which to prepare students for the future! In addition, there is little reason to accept the basic premise of the argument that the world is fundamentally competitive. Quite to the contrary, the essential enabling characteristic of our society is cooperation, not competition. Arthur Combs (1957) made the point well when he stated,

> We are impressed by the competitive features of our society and like to think of ourselves as essentially a competitive people. Yet we are thoroughly and completely dependent upon the goodwill and cooperation of millions of our fellow men . . . . [E]ach of us must rely on others to carry out the tasks we cannot perform ourselves. Although it is true we occasionally compete with others, competition is not the rule of life but the exception. Competition

makes the news, while cooperation sup-
plies the progress. (p. 265)

Moreover, something Combs did not refer to, of equal
importance to cooperation, is being *competent*. On those
occasions when one must compete with others in situations of scarcity—when, say, there are more applicants than
jobs—the only assurance that advocates of teaching competition can give is that by learning to outwit one's classmates, it will be someone else, and not oneself, who loses
out in the future. Obviously, the purpose of schools is not
to train for such "cut-throat" rivalry, and schools cannot
insure their graduates against losing jobs due to seasonal
variations in employment, to economic downturns, or to
technological change. Rather, one purpose of schooling is
to arm students with the skills to cope with unemploy-
ment, whatever its causes, and to increase the students'
chances for a productive life. In this latter regard, being
employable usually depends less on outperforming others
than on being competent, and becoming competent is unlikely when the reasons for learning are competitive.

1 Which of these obstacles to change do you consider more difficult to overcome in your own classroom, and why?

2 What other obstacles come to mind when thinking about your own classroom experiences?

3 What strategies could you use to overcome these obstacles?

SUMMARY

In this section we have considered the obstacles to transforming an ability to an equity game, a process which obviously is neither easy nor simple. The guidelines and theory we propose in this book provide a general blueprint for change, and the obstacles and issues discussed here will help prepare teachers in advance for the challenges ahead. But even with general guidelines, the specifics of change on a day-to-day basis must necessarily be left to the individual teacher.

final review

Revisiting Ms. Jackson's Classroom

Now that we have described the educational benefits of an equity game and suggested ways to initiate it, we return to Ms. Jackson's classroom for a final look. We ask you to imagine that—having read this book—Ms. Jackson decided to convert her earlier teaching approach to one based on an equity game. As a result of this change, the behavior of most of her students has also changed to varying degrees, and for the better. This transformation is well represented in the lives of Noel, Sean, Lydia, and Michael. The following four scenarios are realistic and not entirely hypothetical, because the reactions portrayed here reflect the behavior of various real-life students in Karen's class after she introduced an equity game.

NOEL

As mentioned earlier, Noel was afraid of getting poor grades, but ironically she sabotaged her chances of doing well by procrastinating. What Noel feared more than poor grades was the implication of doing poorly—that she was incompetent, hence unworthy. By procrastinating, Noel could attribute her failures to causes other than low ability, such as not having enough time.

Once Ms. Jackson introduced an equity game, Noel's fear of failure gradually subsided because getting good grades was now within her grasp. Her sense of worth as a student no longer depended on a false notion of her ability compared to that of others. Noel's sense of worth became more connected to her own efforts and self-improvement. Moreover, Noel also responded well to the choice of learning activities now available in Ms. Jackson's classroom and to the different ways Noel could complete these assignments. She especially enjoyed those opportunities to show what she had learned by drawing on her vivid imagination and artistic talent.

Because of the constant validation of Noel's efforts by Ms. Jackson, the negative energy previously fueled by Noel's fears was transformed into enthusiasm, perseverance, and the desire to do her very best. Over the course of the year, Noel's grade went from a "C" in the first quarter to an "A" in the second, third, and fourth quarters. A major improvement!

SEAN

Like Noel, Sean also feared failure. However, for Sean, it was fear and the need to be perfect that motivated him to work so hard, unlike Noel, who avoided work so she would have an excuse for failing. Although Sean's grades did not improve under an equity system—he was already doing exceptionally well, given his preoccupation with grades—his reasons for learning did change. Sean stopped worrying about the possibility of falling short of perfection because he no longer saw perfection as the measure of his worth. The rules of the equity game rewarded behaviors other than outperforming everyone, including recognition for discovering ideas on his own, encouraging risk-taking rather than being perfect, and setting up manageable challenges. Sean was now free to achieve for the sake of curiosity and for self-mastery. These reasons were considerably different from those that motivated Sean in an ability game—and much healthier.

LYDIA

While Noel and Sean were trying to negotiate an ability game so they would look as smart as possible, Lydia had given up playing by these rules, largely because she believed them to be unfair. For years she had tried her very best, but had received little recognition because, try as she might, other students still did better. To Lydia this was frustrating and unfair. As a result, Lydia became withdrawn, even sullen, and mistrusted school and most of her teachers. She rarely turned in assignments and studied little for tests. When Ms. Jackson converted to an equity approach, Lydia had a much longer period of adjustment than did either Noel or Sean. She remained skeptical about the changes and continued for a time in her initial pattern of indifference. Since Lydia was not responding to the many new learning opportunities being offered, Ms. Jackson contacted Lydia's mother, explained the different aspects of the equity game, and urged that Lydia's mother encourage her daughter to take advantage of these opportunities. Shortly thereafter Lydia began completing an assignment or two, a few at a time, and as her grades improved so did her attitude towards school, which reflected a more confident, enthusiastic student. As Lydia improved, Ms. Jackson remarked on the quality of her work, which seemed to encourage Lydia even more. Lydia had begun to put aside the anger at feeling that she had been unfairly treated, because now she could do her best and still be recognized, irrespective of the fact that other students were doing well also.

MICHAEL

As will be recalled, Michael also demonstrated a demoralized pattern of behavior similar to that of Lydia. He was frequently tardy or absent, and generally apathetic toward most schoolwork. In conversations with other students and with Ms. Jackson, Michael was emphatic about his lack of interest in school and talked about how much more relevant life outside of school seemed to him. Behind these attitudes was Michael's firm belief that trying hard in school made no difference, which led him to choose to abandon academic pursuits in favor of outside activities that held far more promise for a sense of belonging. No wonder, then, that Michael showed little interest in playing by the new rules of an equity game because he had basically given up on school. Even calls home, which were met with clear support by Michael's grandmother, had very little impact on his willingness to change his ways. However, Ms. Jackson refused to give up on Michael, because for reasons still unclear to her, from time to time Michael actually completed assignments and did high-quality work that demonstrated heretofore unknown abilities. Nonetheless, as the year ended, with these few positive exceptions, Michael's overall performance had improved little. Michael's case illustrates that for especially disheartened students, growth under an equity game may be very gradual. In these instances change requires great patience and encouragement from both teachers and family.

CONCLUDING THOUGHTS

In this volume, we have proposed an innovative incentive system in which students are encouraged to learn for the sake of learning. In an equity game, students compete only with their own abilities, limitations, and motivations; therefore, the challenge in an equity system is to promote individual competence rather than to foster competition with other students for grades. We believe this system goes a long way toward encouraging students' will to learn, to improve their self-confidence, and, in the long run, to make a teacher's job more rewarding.

As you have seen, this is not a system that requires drastic infrastructural change in order to be instituted. It need not be implemented on a systemwide or schoolwide scale in order to work. What the equity system does require is a different way of thinking on the part of individual teachers about the most successful ways to motivate students, which would result in changes in the reasons for learning in their classrooms.

glossary

Ability game: Dynamic in classrooms in which the rules of achievement reward students for outperforming other students; emphasizes performance per se and high test scores for their own sake.

Absolute or merit-based criteria: A way of measuring the quality of one's performance in absolute terms, irrespective of how many other students do well or poorly.

Academic wooden leg: A self-serving strategy in which an individual admits to a minor personal weakness, like fear of test-taking, in order to avoid acknowledging a greater feared weakness such as inability.

Contingency contracts: Work contracts set up between individual students and teachers for which the grades or other payoffs are contingent on the successful completion of the contract.

Custom testing: A procedure by which students themselves select the difficulty of the test questions they must answer.

Disidentification: A process by which individuals, particularly students of color, distance themselves from the middle-class values and expectations that dominate school life.

Divergent thinking: A type of thinking that involves searching for a diversity of ideas, speculating, and going off in different mental directions while suspending assumptions about present realities and exploring unlikely but not illogical possibilities.

Entity theory of ability: A view of the nature of ability as an immutable capacity of largely genetic origin that is unresponsive to instruction or improvement.

Equity game: Dynamic in classrooms in which the rules of achievement reward students for self-improvement, diligence, and making progress—yardsticks of success that are open to all.

Extrinsic motivation: Reasons for learning that involve the performance of some action, not out of any intrinsic (internal) satisfaction derived from the action itself—like satisfying one's curiosity—but rather for the sake of extrinsic payoffs such as grades or gold stars.

Failure-avoiders: Students who attempt to avoid failure, or at least the implication of failure—that they are unable—by using self-serving strategies such as procrastination, which allows them to blame failure on other factors outside their control.

Incremental theory of ability: A belief about the nature of ability that assumes that one's capacity is an expandable set of skills that improve and grow through experience and instruction.

Intrinsic motivation: The tendency to engage in activities for their own sake, just for the pleasure derived from performing them, such as satisfying one's curiosity.

Mini-max principle: The theory that students attempt to maximize rewards with a minimum of effort.

Motivation: A concept that explains the why of human behavior: Why do individuals and groups act the way they do? Applied to education, motivation refers to the reasons that students learn.

Motivational equity: A condition in which all students, irrespective of ability and background, share common or equal reasons for learning.

Overstrivers: Students who avoid failure by succeeding. Unfortunately, for overstrivers even extraordinary successes do little to resolve doubts about their ability because their goal is not merely doing well, but attaining perfection.

Policy of intensification: A strategy for school reform that proposes establishing more rigorous national achievement standards and holding teachers accountable for attaining them.

Premack principle: The use of an activity preferred by a student as a reward (e.g., free time at the computer) for completing a task that is less attractive to the student.

Procrastination: A self-serving strategy in which individuals postpone studying until the last moment in an effort to blame failure on a lack of preparation, rather than on low ability.

Self-worth dynamics: A theory suggesting that students are driven to achieve success and to avoid failure in order to promote a sense of personal worth; gaining the approval of others as a mark of one's value.

Sham effort: A self-serving strategy in which students appear to be participating in classroom activities, but more in an effort to avoid having to try (and hence not risking failure) than out of any genuine interest in learning.

Task analysis: The process by which students analyze work assignments to determine what makes them difficult for the individual and then take steps to overcome these potential problems.

Token economy: A contractual arrangement by which students are guaranteed certain rewards (e.g., points, grades, or gold stars) for satisfactorily completing various assignments or tasks.

references

Abt, C. C. (1987). *Serious games*. New York: Lanham.

Alexander, K. A., & McDill, E. L. (1976). Selection and allocation within schools: Some causes and consequences of curriculum placement. *American Sociological Review, 41,* 969–980.

Allen, B. V. (1975). Paying students to learn. *Personnel & Guidance Journal, 53*(10), 774–778.

Alschuler, A. S. (1969). The effects of classroom structure on achievement motivation and academic performance. *Educational Technology, 9,* 19–21.

Alschuler, A. S. (1973). *Developing achievement motivation in adolescents*. Englewood Cliffs, NJ: Educational Technology Publications.

Ames, C. (1984). Achievement attributions and self-instructions under competitive and individualistic goal structures. *Journal of Educational Psychology, 76,* 478–487.

Ames, C., & Archer, J. (1987). Mothers' beliefs about the role of ability and effort in school learning. *Journal of Educational Psychology, 79,* 409–414.

Armstrong, T. (1994). *Multiple intelligences in the classroom.* Alexandria, VA: Association for Supervision and Curriculum Development.

Beery, R. G. (1975). Fear of failure in the student experience. *Personnel and Guidance Journal, 54,* 190–203.

Birney, R. C., Burdick, H., & Teevan, R. C. (1969). *Fear of failure.* New York: Van Nostrand.

Butler, R. (1988). Enhancing and undermining intrinsic motivation: The effects of task-involving and ego-involving evaluation on interest and performance. *British Journal of Educational Psychology, 58,* 1–14.

Butler, R. (1993). What young people want to know when: Effects of mastery and ability goals on interest in different kinds of social comparisons. *Journal of Personality and Social Psychology, 62,* 934–943.

Butler, R., & Nisan, M. (1986). Effects of no feedback, task-related comments, and grade on intrinsic instruction and performance. *Journal of Educational Psychology, 78,* 210–216.

Cohen, J., & Filipczak, J. (1971). *A new learning environment.* San Francisco: Jossey-Bass.

Combs, A. W. (1957). The myth of competition. *Childhood Education.* Washington, DC: Association for Childhood Education International.

Covington, M. V. (1986). Instruction in problem solving and planning. In S. L. Friedman, E. K. Skolnick, & R. R.

Cocking (Eds.), *Blueprints for thinking: The role of planning in cognitive development* (pp. 469–511). New York: Cambridge University Press.

Covington, M. V. (1992). *Making the grade: A self-worth perspective on motivation and school reform.* New York: Cambridge University Press.

Covington, M. V., & Beery, R. G. (1976). *Self-worth and school learning.* New York: Holt, Rinehart & Winston.

Covington, M. V., Crutchfield, R. S., Davies, L. B., & Olton, R. M. (1974). *The productive thinking program: A course in learning to think.* Address inquiries to: Professor Martin Covington, Psychology Department, 3210 Tolman Hall, University of California, Berkeley, CA 94720.

Covington, M. V., & Omelich, C. L. (1979). Effort: The double-edged sword in school achievement. *Journal of Educational Psychology, 71,* 169–182.

Covington, M. V., Teel, K. M., & Parecki, A. D. (1994, April). Motivation benefits of improved academic performance among middle-school African-American students through an effort-based grading system. Paper presented at the annual meeting of the American Educational Research Association, New Orleans.

Covington, M.V., & Wiedenhaupt, S. (1996). Turning work into play: The nature and nurturing of intrinsic task engagement. In R. Perry (Ed.), *Higher education: Handbook of theory and research* [Special edition]. New York: Agathon.

Cruikshank, D. R., Telfer, R. A., Ezell, E., & Manford, R. (1987). *Simulations and games: An ERIC bibliography.* Washington, DC: U.S. Dept. of Education.

Daly, M. D., Jacob, S., King, D. W., & Cheramine, G. (1984). The accuracy of teacher predictions of student reward preferences. *Psychology in the Schools, 21,* 520–524.

de Charms, R. (1957). Affiliation motivation and productivity in small groups. *Journal of Abnormal and Social Psychology, 55,* 222–226.

de Charms, R. (1972). Personal causation training in the schools. *Journal of Applied Social Psychology, 2,* 95–113.

Deci, E. L., & Ryan, R. M. (1985). *Intrinsic Motivation and Self-Determination in Human Behavior.* New York: Plenum.

Dewey, J. (1938/1963). *Experience and education.* New York: Collier.

Dweck, C. S., & Bempechat, J. (1983). Children's theories of intelligence: Consequences for learning. In S. G. Paris, G. M. Olson, & H. M. Stevenson (Eds.), *Learning and motivation in the classroom* (pp. 239–256). Hillsdale, NJ: Erlbaum.

Gardner, H. (1993). *Multiple intelligences: The theory and practice.* New York: Basic Books.

Gardner, J. W. (1961). *Excellence: Can we be equal and excellent too?* New York: Harper & Row.

Graham, S. (1988). Can attribution theory tell us something about motivation in Blacks? *Educational Psychologist, 23,* 3–21.

Harari, O., & Covington, M. V. (1981). Reactions to achievement behavior from a teacher and student perspective: A developmental analysis. *American Educational Research Journal, 18,* 15–28.

Harter, S. (1981). A model of mastery motivation in children: Individual differences and developmental change. In A. Pick (Ed.), *Minnesota Symposium on Child Psychology* (Vol. 14). Hillsdale, NJ: Erlbaum.

Haycock, K., & Navarro, M. S. (1988, May). *Unfinished business: Fulfilling our children's promise.* A report from The Achievement Council, 1016 Castro Street, Oakland, CA 94607.

Kaplan, R. M., & Swant, S. G. (1973). Reward characteristics in appraisal of achievement behavior. *Representative Research in Social Psychology, 4*, 11–17.

Kennedy, W. A., & Willcutt, H. C. (1964). Praise and blame as incentives. *Psychological bulletin, 62*, 323–332.

Kohn, A. (1986). *No contest: The case against competition.* Boston: Houghton Mifflin.

Lepper, M. R., & Greene, D. (Eds.). (1978). *The hidden costs of reward: New perspectives on the psychology of human motivation.* Hillsdale, NJ: Erlbaum.

McCombs, B. L. (1984). Process and skills underlying continuing intrinsic motivation to learn: Toward a definition of motivational skills training interventions. *Educational Psychologist, 19*, 199–218.

Mettee, D. R. (1971). Rejection of unexpected success as a function of the negative consequences of accepting success. *Journal of Personality and Social Psychology, 17*, 332–341.

National Academy of Sciences Panel on Secondary School Education for the Changing Workplace (1984). *High school and the changing workplace, the employer's view.* Washington, DC: National Academy Press.

Neimark, E., Slotnick, N. S., & Ulrich, T. (1971). The development of memorization strategies. *Developmental Psychology, 5*, 427–432.

Oakes, J. (1987, October). *Improving inner-city schools: Current directions in urban district reform.* The State University of New Jersey, Rutgers, and the Rand Corporation.

Page, E. (1958). Teacher comments and student performance. *Journal of Educational Psychology, 49*, 173–181.

Pittman, T. S., Boggiano, A. K., & Ruble, D. N. (1983). Intrinsic and extrinsic motivational orientations: Interactive effect of reward, competence feedback, and task complexity. In J. Levine & M. Wang (Eds.), *Teacher and student perceptions: Implications for learning* (pp. 319–340). Hillsdale, NJ: Erlbaum.

Rocklin, T., & O'Donnell, A. M. (1986, September). Self-adapted testing: A performance-improving variant of computerized adaptive testing. Poster session presented at the annual meeting of the American Psychological Association, Washington, DC.

Rosenholtz, S. J., & Wilson, B. (1980). The effect of classroom structure on shared perceptions of ability. *American Educational Research Journal, 17,* 75–82.

Russell, W. J. (1988). Editorial: Presidential campaigns and educational policy. *Educational Researcher, 17*(2), 4, 12.

Sansone, C., Weir, C., Harpster, L., and Morgan, C. (1992). Once a boring task always a boring task? Interest as a self-regulatory mechanism. *Journal of Personality and Social Psychology, 63,* 379–390.

Schoenfeld, A. H. *On mathematics as sense making: An informal attack on the unfortunate divorce of formal and informal mathematics.* Paper presented at OERI/LRCD Conference on Informal Reasoning and Education, Pittsburgh, PA.

Sears, P. S. (1940). Levels of aspiration in academically successful and unsuccessful children. *Journal of Abnormal and Social Psychology, 35,* 498–536.

Slavin, R. E. (1987). Ability grouping and student achievement in elementary schools: A best-evidence synthesis. *Review of Educational Research, 57,* 293–336.

Sofia, J. P. (1978). *The influence of specific goal setting conferences on achievement, attributional patterns and goal setting behavior of elementary school boys.* Unpublished doctoral dissertation, University of California at Berkeley.

Stack, C. B. (1974). *All our kin: Strategies for survival in a Black community.* New York: Harper & Row.

Steele, C. M. (1988). The psychology of self-affirmation: Sustaining the integrity of the self. In L. Berkowitz (Ed.), *Advances in experimental social psychology* (Vol. 21, pp. 261–302). New York: Academic Press.

Suls, J. M., & Miller, R. L. (Eds.). (1977). *Social comparison processes: Theoretical and empirical perspectives*. Washington, DC: Hemisphere.

Teel, K. M. (1995). *Report to the Spencer Foundation: The motivational consequences of improved performance among "low-achieving" African-American students.* Unpublished manuscript.

Teel, K. M., Covington, M. V., & Parecki, A. D. (1996). Promoting a psychological shift in motivation among middle school students. *Journal of Educology*.

Teel, K. M., Parecki, A. D., & Covington, M. V. (1992, April). *Addressing achievement motivation among at-risk African-American middle school students: Implications for curricular changes*. Paper presented at the annual meeting of the American Educational Research Association, San Francisco, CA.

Teel, K. M., Parecki, A. D., & Covington, M. V. (1993, April). *Addressing achievement motivation among at-risk African-American middle school students: A collaborative attempt to apply theory to practice*. Paper presented at the annual meeting of the American Educational Research Association, Atlanta, GA.

Toufexis, A. (1989, May 1). Report cards can hurt you. *Time*, 75.

Weinstein, R. S. (1981, April). Student perspectives on achievement in varied classroom environments. In P. Blumenfeld (Chair), *Student perspectives and the study of the classroom*. Symposium conducted at the meeting of the American Educational Research Association, Los Angeles, CA.

Woodson, C. E. (1975). Motivational effects of two-stage testing. Unpublished manuscript, Institute of Human Learning, University of California, Berkeley.

ABOUT THE AUTHORS

Martin V. Covington is professor of psychology at the University of California, Berkeley. Professor Covington's areas of research focus on the psychology of creativity, the development of curricula to promote academic problem-solving skills, and the investigation of fear-of-failure dynamics and test anxiety in schools. Professor Covington is senior author of the *Productive Thinking Program,* a course in learning to think developed for elementary school students. He is a recipient of the Berkeley Distinguished Teaching Award, and is past president of the International Society for Test Anxiety Research.

Karen M. Teel has been a classroom teacher in the West Contra Costa school district for 25 years. She received her doctorate in education from the University of California at Berkeley in 1993 and has been a classroom teacher–researcher at Portola Middle School for 4 years. She is the current president of the Teacher as Researcher special interest group of the American Educational Research Association. Dr. Teel's research interests are achievement motivation, urban schools, and teacher research. In 1994, Dr. Teel was the recipient of a 2-year Spencer postdoctoral fellowship to continue her classroom research.